The PLAYSKOOL™

Guide to Baby Play

More Than 300 Games and Activities to Play and Learn with Your Baby

Robin McClure

SOURCEBOOKS, INC.®
NAPERVILLE, ILLINOIS

Published by Sourcebooks, Inc.

P.O. Box 4410, Naperville, Illinois 60567-4410
(630) 961-3900
Fax: (630) 961-2168
www.sourcebooks.com

Library of Congress Cataloging-in-Publication Data

McClure, Robin.
  The Playskool guide to baby play : 500 games you can play-and-learn with your baby / Robin McClure.
    p. cm.
  ISBN-13: 978-1-4022-1069-3 (pbk.)
  ISBN-10: 1-4022-1069-8 (pbk.)
  1. Infants-Development. 2. Play. 3. Parent and infant. I. Title.

HQ774.M44 2007
649'.55-dc22
                          2007029263

Printed and bound in the United States of America.
     BG 10 9 8 7 6 5 4 3 2 1

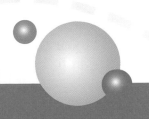

Contents

About This Book

Oh baby, baby! There's so much to see and do and everyone is so excited to have you join the family! But after the announcements have been sent, congratulations extended, and the nursery prepared, what can mom and dad "do" with their seemingly fragile and helpless newborn beyond tending to baby's basic needs? Plenty! Here are more than 300 loving and interactive ways new parents (and doting grandparents) can bond and play with the tiniest member of the family as baby blossoms and thrives in the first year. Keep in mind that parents are baby's first teacher . . . every day there is a new lesson plan of fun and learning!

Acknowledgments

When seeking inspiration for this book, I looked no further than into the innocent eyes of some incredibly unique babies whom I have had the privilege of getting to know—and yes, hold and cuddle! I also pulled out all my treasured scrapbooks and baby mementos and spent considerable quiet time reflecting on the first year of life of my own three children, relishing in the poignant memories that ultimately brought unexpected tears of joy and even sadness for personal baby times now past.

I hold dear to my heart baby treasures that include first diapers, first teeth, first locks of hair, and first footprints. Looking at them from time to time resurrects overwhelmingly tender feelings of a time when my life was consumed with sweet (and not-so-sweet) smells of baby, lingering looks of total adoration and trust, and moments when time existed for me to simply take in the incredulous feeling that my husband, Rick, and I were responsible for such a tiny miracle. While my precious brood (Hunter, Erin, and Connor) are still at home, I realize that time will quickly pass and they will soon be grown—and then I will only relive these blessed times through new babies of family, close friends, neighbors, and someday, grandchildren.

I believe it is true that the firstborn benefits the most from parental doting and experiences, but perhaps not in the way it may seem. I know now that *all* newborns are "firstborns" because of their uniqueness. With each of my precious children, my husband and I ventured down an unknown path of "firsts." Any milestone for our oldest was no more or less special than the first achievement for our third. There are no repeats with kids; no "same ol' routine." Smiles and giggles are different, as are cries, eating habits, and even preferred mode of mobility. (I had one early walker, a cruiser, and one full-blown crawler, for example.) There are many routes to choose in the journey of parenting, and in the end, it seems that the paths parents choose with a baby's first year lead to well-adjusted and happy children. Isn't that what makes it such a grand adventure?

Introduction

You Have a Baby! Now What?

Whether you are first-time parents or seasoned moms and dads, anticipating the arrival of a baby involves months of waiting, dreaming, making plans, going on doctor's appointments, and preparing for the "big day" of arrival. But after the grand arrival reality sets in. Congratulations . . . you have a baby! Now what?

Every newborn is unique, and as a result, getting to know your infant is a new experience, regardless of whether it is your first or fifth baby, or somewhere in between. At birth a newborn can respond to variations in temperature, texture, pleasure, and pain. He recognizes his parents' voices and has strong survival reflexes in place. An infant may also have strong preferences from the very beginning, such as whether or not she likes to be bundled, how she prefers to be held, or how loud or soft she likes to be spoken to. Many also have particular food preferences if using formula versus taking nourishment from the breast. As such, every new addition to a family means parents are brand-new to this particular experience. Getting to know your newborn, and having baby get to know you, takes time, effort, patience, and lots of trial and error!

Many well-intended references have been made about newborns being a helpless "blob" (the word choice affectionately used by actress Angelina Jolie when discussing her daughter Shiloh as a newborn) or a fragile "bundle," mainly because it seems on the surface that infants just eat, sleep, and, well, poop! But, while their physical abilities are quite limiting at first, their budding brains are anything but! Each new experience spurs an incredible development and growth at a remarkable speed. And all the loving parent-baby interactions that take place that first year contribute to the amazing transition from newborn, to infant, to baby, to toddler . . . all in just one incredible, whirlwind-paced year!

Normal activities help to develop a baby's growth, heighten senses, and spur development. A loving, nurturing environment only aids in this growth through the promotion of early learning. But enriching and loving activities done together as family can also be a lot of fun; sometimes the sweetest and most precious memories are built on tender caresses, a first year of "firsts," and those poignant smiles and trials.

While parents sometimes are bombarded with well-meaning, yet unsolicited, advice and tips on raising a child, this book embraces the notion that parents in their hearts truly know what's best for their newborn and family. This book is intended to provide some inspiration, family fun, and memorable moments that all come with the fabulous first year of raising a baby. As you read through these activities, keep in mind that all babies develop at different paces, so if yours isn't ready or shows no interest in something today, try it again in a few weeks. You'll often be astonished at how much your precious one has already changed and developed!

Parents and caregivers should also keep in mind that anything that catches a baby's eye for play can be considered an educational experience. It's true that there are some really cool toys and products on the market; however, they are certainly not necessary for a baby's development or brain growth! Case in point: watch your baby open a present from a gift bag. Undoubtedly, he will find the bag, tissue paper, and bows as much fun, if not more, than the contents inside. While parents certainly can augment their child's learning experiences with toys and items touted as educational, they should keep in mind that good ol' fashioned free play, combined with lots of love and interaction, is what a baby most needs for development.

Time truly flies during the first year of your baby's life! Cherish each stage and the opportunity to play and get to know your unique little being whose personality and preferences are emerging before your very eyes. Slow down and enjoy each milestone. Before you know it, you'll have a toddler!

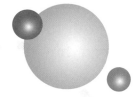

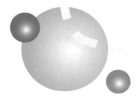

Welcome to the World!

Games and activities for birth to 3 months

From simple fun and games to exaggerated gestures, to watching movements and listening to sounds, your precious one is ready for some early fun!

Sometimes it's hard to say who learns more in the first months of a newborn's life at home—parents or baby. Figuring out sleeping patterns and general hygiene such as sponge baths and umbilical cord care is one thing, but beyond that, it's time to get *really* up close and personal with your infant! Touch is typically a newborn's most highly developed sense at birth, so hugging, touching, and caressing your baby is essential for bonding and for making him safe, secure, and loved. These simple interactions also help promote recognition.

From coos, gurgles, and yes, toothless smiles, to other wordless expressions, your infant at two months has communications on the mind. Moms and dads can delight in those early sweet sounds and begin encouraging verbal exchanges, recognition, and early communication.

By the three month mark, your baby is settling in to life, and is more alert and awake than ever. This means it's show time! From simple fun and games to exaggerated gestures that are mimicked, to watching movements and listening to sounds, your precious one is ready for some early fun!

Seeing

Hello family!

Babies are capable of learning from birth, so introduce baby to her new family members now and show her around her new home. Create quality "get-to-know-you" time where you and baby do nothing but look into each other's eyes and say hello. You can also gently rock your baby while you closely gaze at her (remember, she can't see well or far at this stage), and encourage her to focus and take in the folks she'll be calling family!

As a way to get comfortable holding your newborn, give her a home tour. Talk to her while walking through the home, pausing to let her take in lights and colors. Repeat the home tour regularly throughout the first month to familiarize baby with her new surroundings. Soon her eyes will gain the ability to focus on objects and patterns.

If baby has older siblings, you'll find that she will love to watch their seemingly endless activity. After baby adjusts to her home, place her in safe positions where she can easily observe her brother or sister in action. Newborns are typically able to follow or track an object in the first few weeks of life, so encourage her to track you! Talk to your baby, get up close and personal, and then walk in both directions and offer praise as she follows you with her eyes.

Unless the weather is extreme, take your newborn outdoors after she is two to three weeks old for an outdoor orientation. Make sure to shield her sensitive eyes and skin from direct sunlight, and then let her feel the wind, experience warmth or coolness (within moderation), and get a first sight of the outdoor world.

Furry friends

Pets need time to adjust to a new addition to the family (after all, pets are often the "baby" until the new bundle arrives home from the hospital). Be sure to safely introduce pets to the new baby, and make sure your pet feels comfortable. Let your newborn and your pet safely look at each other, and as the comfort level grows, let them smell and gently touch one another. Your baby will most likely find your pet a constant source of entertainment as she grows older! Never leave your pet unsupervised with your newborn. They'll have plenty of time to get to know and to trust each other.

Watch me, baby!

Your newborn's eyes are capable of vision, but his brain typically isn't mature enough for him to distinguish between colors and shapes. Simple finger games such as the "Itsy Bitsy Spider" don't need any props and can be impromptu fun for you and baby both.

Or, if you're ready to get really silly, bob your head up and down and in each direction while your baby is watching you to encourage him to follow your movements.

Ball juggle

Juggle a small ball or play catch with yourself, and encourage your baby to watch the ball's movement with his eyes. Tell your newborn that you're throwing the ball into the air and catching it in your hands, and be sure to show excitement each time you make a catch.

Upward gaze

Place your newborn in a room with a ceiling fan above, and turn it on while you stand nearby. The movement will attract your baby's gaze, the whir of the blades will calm him, and the gentle breeze will also feel good on his skin.

Soft Lights for Baby

Consider adding small twinkle lights in a soft color to your infant's nursery, or installing adjustable bright rope lights on shelving or along a high wall that is safely out of reach. The soft colors are pleasing to the eye and interesting to baby, while providing much-needed nighttime light for mom and dad. Get a timer so you can easily control when the lights are on and off.

Extreme contrast

There is an abundance of baby toys on the market that feature high-contrast color schemes (think of black/white/red patterns, for example), but you can also show baby high-contrast colors as you walk around your home. Create items of visual interest by placing a black phone on a white piece of paper, or showing baby a photo in a black frame that has a white border. Your baby will be most interested in your voice as you show her these items, but will also be interested in looking at the items with you.

You can even use black and red marker on white paper and create some flashcard designs. They can be as simple as tic-tac-toe designs, stars, or circles. Mom and dad can place baby in a safe laid-back style seat and show him some shapes and patterns that are certain to get a second glance.

Look and laugh

Your newborn has discovered the fun of smiling and laughing. People smile at her and she smiles back, which causes even bigger smiles, and so on. This smiling game can be never-ending fun, with every smile a greater joy and bigger reaction.

Play a simple game of "look and laugh" where you and your baby look at each other and then break into exaggerated laughter. Your baby will love hearing your deep belly-laughs, and she will find watching you having so much fun an absolute hoot.

Open and close

Introduce your baby to the concepts of open and close. An easy demonstration is a kitchen cabinet. Show baby "open" and then show "close." As your baby's development continues, let her open and close a cabinet herself!

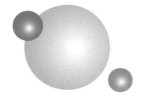

Paper peek-a-boo

Draw a simple face with a silly expression on a sheet of paper and hold it in front of your face. Then, pull it away quickly while saying "peek-a-boo, guess who?" Your baby will see that it's *you* behind the paper. Change your expression each time you pull the paper away to hold baby's interest longer.

Heads up

Your infant is no longer a weeble-wobble newborn, and he can now hold his head up for prolonged periods of time. Encourage the strengthening of those neck muscles by holding him upright and letting him view the world. Say, "Heads up, Baby! Look at that car!" and talk to your youngster about things that may hold his gaze (even briefly).

Lie on your stomach while your infant does the same and have "in your face" conversations. Encourage baby to lift his head upward while making eye contact with you to help build his neck muscles.

Marvelous me!

Your baby's favorite person—after mom and dad, of course—is himself! Give him a child-safe mirror (most toys feature unbreakable mirrors) so he can check himself out. He will also enjoy watching himself as he is being bathed or groomed in the bathroom mirror.

Flap Books

Your infant is at an ideal age for looking at simple board books with flaps or textures. You may need to show baby how to look behind a flap or to touch a certain texture, but before long, he will have mastered this on his own. Try to read to your infant daily!

Flower power

Let your infant smell a flower while you are on a stroll outdoors, or hold one in your hand for him to examine. Pick a fragrant flower that he will certainly note, such as freesia or a gardenia, if possible. Don't let him touch it; looking and smelling is best at this age.

Dangling objects

Baby can now use his eyes to follow a toy or item of interest from side to side. Entertain him by dangling a small stuffed animal or toy that makes sounds on one side of him and then the other and watch him follow. Talk about the hopping frog animal or the dancing ballerina while you move it from side to side to further capture your newborn's interest.

Hang items at a safe distance above baby's changing table that will capture his attention. You can simply perch a small stuffed animal above or hang items that move or dangle. It's a great way to calm an active baby enough to get those diapers changed without any howls!

Baby's Vision is Still Developing

Your baby can see better to either side rather than straight ahead at this stage, so don't hang a mobile directly over her just yet. Instead, put it on the side of a crib or find objects that baby can look at peripherally.

Hearing

Listening in

Hearing is fully developed in full-term newborns, so don't forget that baby will be listening in! Early evidence of this is the fact that most infants will briefly stop moving when they hear sound at a conversational level. Try it with your little one: start a normal-tone conversation, watch baby's reaction, and then stop. Repeat and observe your newborn's reaction.

Babies will also respond to the pitch of the voice they hear. Newborns seem to prefer a higher-pitched voice (mom's) to a deeper voice (dad's), so help baby get used to dad's voice by singing in high pitches as well as low pitches. Encourage dad to talk regularly when holding the baby or interacting with the baby. If she seems to dislike dad's voice, have him speak in a higher pitch and softly at first.

To help your baby get accustomed to the sound of her own name, as well as the sound of your voice, improvise some silly sing-song melodies with your newborn's name. Don't worry about the tune or even the lyrics; sing songs like "Silly, silly Sarah" or "Ethan, my Ethan. How I love you so."

As a way to transition your infant to normal family noises and activities, consider placing a monitor in reverse so that your baby can hear the family talk and laugh.

House sounds

While holding your baby, begin to introduce him to the sounds he'll hear around the house. Tell him about the telephone as it rings, show him how the doorbell rings and sounds; let him listen to the dog's bark or a cat's purr. Be sure to identify each sound as it is made. Your infant may be only just starting to experience the world, but this is how babies begin to learn and feel comfortable in their growing surroundings.

For some extra special bonding time, place your baby in a sling or carrier and vacuum together. Your newborn may find the noise and repetitive back-and-forth motions calming.

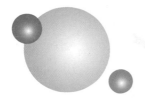

Talk time

Child experts maintain that newborns remember and recognize their mother's voice from their days in the womb, so encourage that continued familiarity and trust by talking out loud throughout the day with your baby. Most of us mentally run through to-do lists each day to keep ourselves organized and focused; try verbally expressing everything you are thinking in a normal voice and in a conversational tone. Spending time alone with baby shouldn't mean simply quiet time or small baby talk. You can talk with your newborn about items you need to buy at the grocery store, about how the house is a mess, and what time dad will be home. It really doesn't matter what you're saying; just say it!

Plan your day, decide what's for dinner, discuss the household with your spouse, or simply talk during routine chores and tasks. Your infant thrives on hearing familiar voices. Some parents make the mistake of keeping baby's environment too quiet. Let your infant be a part of all the family routines to familiarize him with family members and schedules. Let him hear the conversations and the activity-based chaos that sometimes occurs in homes (he'll let you know if it's too stimulating).

Let your baby be an important part of your morning ritual. Use a bouncer or infant seat to let him be near you as you shower, brush your teeth and hair, etc. Tell him everything you're doing and why. Not only will your infant enjoy hearing your voice, he'll likely be interested in the sounds and smells of everything you're doing as well.

Soothing sounds

Babies crave soft, soothing noises, and humming to your baby will comfort her as well as connect her with your loving voice. Hum while changing your newborn, bathing her, and burping her. Play soothing and calm melodies to help heighten a newborn's sense of hearing and to help soothe an irritable baby.

The "Shush Little Baby" nursery rhyme remains popular because it works! Softly rock your newborn while singing this song or simply make the soothing "shush" sound to put her to sleep. This also works to calm restless babies. Noise like static or recordings of rainfall, ocean waves, or other repetitive sounds can calm a baby as well.

Babies don't need total silence in order to sleep; in fact, they are used to hearing sounds from their time in the womb. So, go ahead and make a normal amount of noise during her naps … you may find she sleeps better!

Sleep Cues

Be careful not to "train" an infant to not be able to sleep unless certain noises or environment are maintained.

That's my family!

Record the voices of loved ones using a tape player or other device and play them back for your baby. Capture mom and dad saying goofy things, making sound effects, or singing songs; a sibling's giggles and playful noises; and grandma or grandpa's greetings of hello. You can even include a recording of the family dog barking! Play the recordings for baby while you explain who is talking. You can also play them as a way to calm a fussy baby.

Tick-tock clock

An infant can find a grandfather clock with its frequent chimes, cuckoo bird, or musical melodies absolutely fascinating. Smaller varieties of clocks also exist in which short melodies or silly sounds occur every 15 minutes, half hour, or hourly, depending on the design. Babies will learn to anticipate sounds coming from the clock!

Wind chimes

Find some sweet-sounding wind chimes and let your baby enjoy the sounds on breezy days. Besides watching the movement of the chimes, your infant will find the clanging sounds interesting.

Countdown clues

When you're out of sight but still within hearing distance from your baby, start counting down from 10 to 1. Say, "Dad is going to come kiss you on the count of 10! . . . 10 . . . 9 . . . 8 . . ." Then come closer with each count until you reach 0 and plant some silly kisses on your baby. He'll learn to anticipate the countdown and its end result!

Sweet secrets

Many babies find whispering soothing. When baby is alert, whisper sweet secrets in one ear, and then in the other. Try making soft silly "shhh" and "sppp" sounds and watch his reaction.

New Reactions

By one month of age, your infant should know and react to voices he is familiar with. While reactions may be minimal, watch closely for a response and provide positive reinforcement that you are nearby.

Shakin' it baby, now!

Go ahead, put on some good tunes and don't feel embarrassed shaking it up with baby, twisting and shouting. Your baby may find it absolutely hilarious to watch mom or dad shaking and twisting to music, playing air guitar, and being all around super silly!

Walking stick

Don a type of walking stick (cane, wrapping paper tube, or umbrella, for example), and make it "clank" or "thump" as you walk around the house while holding baby. The new sound will be something that can pique baby's interest in the walks.

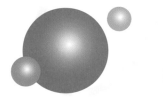

Touch

Hand presses

Your newborn will likely keep her hands curled into a soft fist. Encourage your infant to open up. Press your open hand against her hand by gently opening up her curled fingers and encouraging them to straighten out, so that you are palm to palm. Gently stroke the back of your baby's hand with your other hand for extra sensation!

I Want to Hold Your Hand

Soon enough, you'll be required to hold your tot's hand for safety reasons, but for now just teach your infant to hold hands as a gesture of love and security. Holding hands can be therapeutic and rewarding for an adult, and just noting the size difference fosters that lovin' feeling!

Baby breathing

Nothing is more endearing than to have your tiny newborn curled up on your chest. Match your baby's breathing and breathe in tandem with exaggerated sound. Breathe in and out deeply and let her hear and feel your breathing. Add tender words or sounds and just enjoy the quiet bonding time.

Bathtub fun

Most newborns enjoy a warm-water sponge bath (the soothing sponge and the parent's touch is part of the enjoyment). Mom and dad can do this together, creating a positive family bath-time experience. As baby's eyes gain focus and her vision improves, provide her with a mirror view during bath time so she can begin watching herself and seeing you as well!

Feels good!

Did you know that your newborn's skin is the most highly developed sensory organ at birth? Help your infant adjust to her expansive world by gently stimulating (through simple stroking or rubbing) her arms, legs, belly, back, cheeks, and head. Take time to daily rub your newborn's legs or arms, while looking at her and talking to her. Most newborns crave this kind of interaction and thrive from the stimulation of touch.

Family members can also take turns sharing gentle bear hugs with baby. Safely hold onto your precious one with a big hug while walking around. Each person hugs and holds a baby in a unique way, and your baby may respond to Papa Bear and Momma Bear differently.

Whether your newborn has a head full of hair or is totally bald, use a silky-soft baby brush to gently massage and brush your child's hair. It's not that your infant needs her hair brushed; it's that the sensation and stimulation feels really good!

Calming Fussy Infants

Swaddle your newborn and then gently swing her back and forth in your arms to mimic the womb. This typically helps to calm fussy or agitated infants.

Baby massage

Give your infant a simple foot massage. While having your baby lie flat on his back, lean in so that eye contact can be established, raise a leg and gently caress the foot and toes. You can even add some lotion for an extra special massage!

Applying lotion to your infant can become a soothing ritual that fosters touch across his body. Be sure to get very close (remember, newborns can't see very well), and play baby lullabies while slowly rubbing lotion on your infant's legs, arms, and tummy. Have your partner hold the baby close so you can apply lotion on his back as well.

For a super close connection, lie face-to-face on a bed and breathe slowly and rhythmically while rubbing your baby's back or limbs. Let your infant feel your breath as you inhale and exhale. Maintain close eye contact.

So soft!

Nestle your newborn's face against your own, and slowly sway and move while humming or singing softly to promote bonding and trust.

Let your baby feel super-soft items like a silk scarf or a satin blanket. Why do you think so many babies bond with a soft or silky blanket? This is the time to add a "luvie" to his routine, if desired. It may become an important fixture for the family; many expert moms recommend buying two of the same blanket or other soft items that your baby likes, so you'll have a backup and be able to wash one unnoticed!

Your baby may begin showing an interest in soft toys, with no sharp edges or small parts. Find ones that can be easily washed; it's a sure bet that your baby will want to "mouth" it as well as feel it.

Toe kisser

Toes at this stage are absolutely irresistible! You can turn toe kissing into a fun ritual. Right after bath is a great time to play the toe kissing game. Say, "I'm going to kiss your toes . . . let me kiss those delicious toes!" Then kiss them one at a time as you lightly tickle the feet and count to 10. Your baby will begin anticipating the toe kissing and later he will squeal at the mere mention of it!

Toasty blanket

Warm a blanket in the dryer (make sure it's not too hot) and wrap it around your baby. You can do the same for baby's socks or even clothes, especially after a bath or on a cool day.

Up Close and Personal

Remove your shirt and place baby directly on your chest for warmth, skin-to-skin bonding, and to enjoy the rhythm of baby's heartbeat.

Keyboard clangs

Don't throw away an old computer keyboard; your infant will have a blast pounding on its keys and making the clickety-click sounds. If you dare, let baby sit on your lap and play with a keyboard that is connected. Open a blank document, and let her see what she can create!

Squishy ball

Find some really interesting ball-shaped baby toys that feature squishy, rubbery material. Let your baby touch and play with them (under constant adult supervision). Squishy balls can intrigue infants with their texture and stretchiness.

Put your hand in mine

Your hand is one of the most natural and interesting objects that baby will love to hold. Provide extra interest by wriggling your fingers or softly tickling the inner palm of her hands with your own. A hand is a toy that is always immediately available and able to provide quick entertainment and positive sensations!

Taste and smell

Scent-sational smells

Surround your baby with subtle aromas and watch his reaction. Pass some cut fruit such as a banana, apple, or orange under his nose and watch his reaction. See how he reacts to the smell of cinnamon or vanilla (a small unlit candle contains subtle scent). You can gauge a baby's like or dislike by his expression. Just remember, something he likes or dislikes today may change a few weeks later!

Lip Smack

Babies sometimes smack their lips as a visual cue for nourishment.

Nose knows

While your infant will be surrounded with smells, try to use consistent soap, shampoo, and even deodorant for the first few months, as your baby will be comforted by and connected with the familiar. Provide your baby with a worn shirt from both mom and dad to snuggle with when fussy. Your scents can help calm and comfort.

Your baby already associates certain smells with mom and other loved ones, but at this stage she's secure enough to associate additional smells with other people and outside influences (such as deodorant or cologne). Your baby has strong preferences in scents, and parents can begin cuing in on likes and dislikes. Watch and observe what your baby's nose says about what she smells.

Smells good!

While your baby most likely won't provide you with feedback, allow her to experience some of the good smells that are part of your daily routine. One of the best places to do this is the kitchen, of course! While keeping safety first, of course, let your baby be in the kitchen with you as you brew a fresh pot of coffee or pull cinnamon rolls out of the oven.

Language development

Back talk

Place your baby on his back, and place your face up close and personal next to his (either on all fours over him, or right by his side). Then, encourage some "back talk" by making baby talk in a fun way. Try and excite your baby and promote coos and gurgles . . . the earliest forms of language!

Early language often takes the form of funny noises, and a common one is a tongue click. As your baby starts working the tongue muscle, mimic the clicking sound back and have some close-up, tongue-clicking time! You can also teach your baby the sounds *oooh* and *aahh* (the first pre-words typically uttered by infants), and then encourage him to perfect them through exaggerated *ooohs* and *aahs* of your own.

Take advantage of close and personal times to make really silly sounds, and do over-the-top character impressions to capture your infant's interest and heart! Let it all out . . . there's no problem with being a drama king or queen when your baby is the only audience member.

Rubber duckies

Make "quack quack" sounds while your tot plays with a cute rubber ducky in the bathtub. Try to get him to imitate the duck sound! The squeaky sound of a rubber ducky just promises lots of squeals.

Understanding Those First Vocalizations

Babies cry as their first, and often only, way to communicate. Child experts agree that cries are often different based on a baby's needs or wants. Cue into the sounds of your infant's first vocalizations. Listen to pitch, temperament, and time of day, and you'll become a cry expert in no time!

Pleasure squeals

At this stage, your baby will squeal with extreme pleasure! Have fun at this stage by introducing toys or activities that he will be sure to love, such as allowing him to touch (safely, and with help) the friendly family pet or experience a fan blowing lightly on his face. There will be lots of happy squeals in your child's future, and parents should take advantage of every pleasure squeal opportunity!

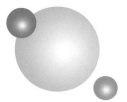

Motor development

Stretch it out

Encourage your newborn to stretch out a bit. Newborns tend to stay curled up because that's how they spent their pre-birth time in the fetal position. While your baby will straighten up as she acclimates to her big new world, you can do some simple, gentle stretching exercises that you'll both enjoy. With your baby flat on her back, raise and lower legs gently in a straight position. Slowly extend her arms over her head. Stop if your baby at any time doesn't like the exercise movements.

Sweet suckles

Observe your newborn's rooting reflex by stroking her cheek or mouth area, and marvel as to how she instinctively turns her mouth toward the sensation and attempts to suckle. This inborn reflex helps a baby find the ever-important food source. A similar reflex is the sucking reflex, in which a baby will suck when something touches the roof of her mouth.

Body roll

Who can miss the frustration on a baby's face when he first attempts to roll over? Your baby will achieve this milestone soon enough, but you can assist his early efforts by placing a rolled-up towel on one side of him as he attempts to roll over, and also by practicing with him to show how it is done. It takes a lot of energy to successfully roll over; even more to roll back.

Every Baby is Different

Almost overnight, your newborn has progressed from a seemingly helpless bundle to one with increasing energy and interest in his world. Some babies discover the ability to roll over from their backs to their sides and then stomachs on their own; others need coaxing.

Stepping out

Of course your infant isn't ready to walk yet, but you can observe a stepping reflex by carefully holding him in a standing position on a level surface. He will make stepping motions, bending the leg at the knee, similar to the movements of early walking.

Moon light

Give your baby a moon light (dome light) to play with at every diaper change. Show your infant how to press it to turn the light on and then press it again to turn it off. At first, your baby most likely will not be able to turn it on and off although she will be fascinated with the concept. Then, without warning, she will suddenly have the strength and will understand the concept of pushing in the dome to make the light turn on. Make the light a toy only to keep her attention during diaper changes. Make sure she has close adult supervision while she plays with the light.

Muscle madness

Infants have a strong grip reflex, so take advantage of it at this stage to stimulate fine and gross motor skills. Use your thumbs as a grip for your baby, and do some fun exercises, such as bending and straightening, making boxing and jabbing motions, and even karate-style maneuvers. Make silly sound effects as you do this to encourage your child.

Your baby is also increasingly showing interest in being in an upright position, so encourage the development of gross motor skills by gently pulling her up from a lying down position to a sitting up position. Wow, the world looks really different from this angle!

Babies will typically kick their feet before they swat with their hands, so you can have fun with baby "leg swats" by dangling something down by your baby's legs and encouraging her to swat or kick at it. Examples can include jangle-type baby toys, a stretchy-ball, a yo-yo, or even things such as a curling ribbon. Place a couple of baby-safe toys that squeak or rattle at the foot of your infant's crib so he can kick at them and make noise. Some baby products feature "kick-oriented" activities that infants enjoy.

Mimic me moments

Newborns quickly learn how to mimic the facial expressions of loved ones. One of the most enjoyable baby-parent experiences is to find a time when baby is happy and alert, and then create some silly or exaggerated features (he'll let you know if he finds the expressions scary) and then watch him react. Try sticking out your tongue and rolling it around while making silly noises, wrinkling your nose, and rolling your eyes. You'll be amazed how quickly your newborn will begin mimicking back!

Playtime is Brain Time, Too

Experts say a baby's brain development is "experience-dependent," meaning that everything your newborn does or experiences can contribute to brain growth. Normal parent-infant interactions spur this growth. Make an effort to have one-on-one "brain" time with your baby through touch, talk, and tender-lovin' care.

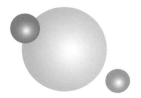

Reach and grab

Encourage your baby to grab dangling toys and large objects within arm's reach. Start with soft items that are easy to grasp and then as your baby develops, progress to more challenging objects, such as blocks.

Standing tall

Begin encouraging your infant to straighten his legs and to "stand up" (with support). A good parent-baby position for practicing this motion is to hold your infant on your lap while seated, facing you. From this position, encourage him to "stand up" and lock those legs straight so that you two can look at each other in the eye. Every time he achieves "standing up," make a different funny face or silly sound to get him to want to repeat it and try it again!

Open hands

Make a game out of having your baby open and close his hands. Have him clinch his hands closed and then open them back up with fingers extended. Show him how to do it with your own hands, and keep him entertained by flashing your digits!

Family fun

Out and about

New parents can get stir-crazy after being housebound for the first few weeks with a newborn. Assuming good health and favorable weather conditions, take your newborn to somewhere quiet outside the home, such as a local library or bookstore, quiet coffee shop, or even a department store during non-peak times.

The motion of a car helps calm a fussy newborn and it can provide relaxation and enjoyment for mom and dad. Go for short, enjoyable car rides to acclimate your infant to the experience and to provide talk time for mom and dad.

If you prefer to get out on foot, introduce your newborn to sights and sounds while on stroller journeys. Most likely, your newborn will sleep through the experience, but she may awaken at times. Marvel with your infant about the surroundings, and talk with her about what you're doing together.

Sights and sounds

Capture the earliest sounds of your infant on a video camera or tape recorder. Those early guttural sounds, sighs of contentment, or even early squeaks and cries will provide precious memories for a lifetime.

Circle dance

Most infants love the motion of slowly going in a circle. Hold your infant in your arms and do a slow-motion circle dance. You can practice your dance moves with your new partner!

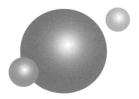

Goofy animals

Act like a silly dog, panting and sniffing, and even barking and howling (but not too loudly, please). Sniff your baby up and down and engage in some loving "dog play!"

Turn your index and middle fingers into bunny ears. While your baby is on his back or during diaper changes, tell your baby that "some bunny's gonna get ya." Make silly hopping or wriggling ear gestures with your fingers, landing on the tummy, and then bouncing up to provide a "bunny kiss" to the cheek!

Restaurant adventure

The earlier you begin eating-out experiences with baby, the more familiar she will be with the sights and sounds of restaurants. Why not take baby for a short dining adventure? Now is the perfect time to begin. Many restaurants have infant seat carriers that allow baby to be safe and nearby the parents while at a restaurant. Plan an outing during off-peak hours and enjoy your couple time.

Single-syllable sing-song

This a perfect stage to have some interactive single-syllable, sing-song fun. Your infant should be attempting some early vocalization, and will often mimic or sing back to you as she is able. Try something simple such as "ba-ba-ba, da-da-da." Raise and lower your pitch while smiling and looking at your baby to coax her into the game.

Pleased to Meet You!

Your infant is beginning to go more places with you now and craves the interaction of being talked to. Introduce your little one to family and friends and encourage them to talk to her directly. Notice how she is becoming increasingly interested in people's faces and happenings.

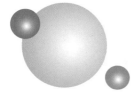

Day at the races

Let baby watch a day at the races with toy cars. Create some simple ramps and then say, "On your mark, get set, and GO!" and let her see which car ends up as the winner, or which one crashes and flips.

Parent stretch and pose

Do some stretching exercises along with your baby. Start by placing your infant on her back on a mat or carpet. Stand over your baby with your legs apart, and then while keeping your knees straight, bend downward to touch and talk with your infant. Stretch yourself from side to side, all the while talking and maintaining eye contact with your baby. She will enjoy watching you move up and down, side to side. If possible, make this a regular ritual, and before long, your baby will want to join in the fun!

Bike riding baby

While baby is on his back, hold his feet and make circular motions like he's riding a bike. Pedal forward, and then pedal backward. Apply the foot brakes, and then start again. You can also add to the fun by doing silly things with his feet such as occasionally criss-crossing legs or going over "bumps" while bicycling. Make up a story about going on a bike ride and talk about what baby encounters along the way.

Huff 'n' puff

Your baby won't be afraid of the big, bad wolf, but instead he will think it's all too funny to watch you huff and puff and blow something away . . . like a tissue! Show your baby how to huff and puff and blow.

Mystery toy

Create a special "mystery bag" for baby (a pillowcase works great) and pull out a mystery toy that he can play with every few days. Simply rotate special toys to keep baby's interest in them; that way, every mystery toy will seem like something new!

Pencil play

Dad and mom can entertain baby by creating simple figures, or puppets, out of everyday objects. A pencil, cell phone, napkin, or fingers can all become impromptu puppets! No need to create facial features; simply have the objects talk to one another with animated voices and silly movements, and he will find your puppet show hilarious! This makes for good entertainment when you're in a situation where there's not much to do or play with.

Dancing Bear's Big Debut

At this stage, your infant prefers objects and toys that move slowly and have a soft, gentle sound. You can create the same effect by playing some soft music and making a stuffed animal dance slowly and sweetly around baby. Remember, silent or fixed objects typically won't hold baby's interest at all . . . at least right now.

Arts and crafts

Feet photo keepsake

Grab your camera and line up the bare feet of all family members in a row (including baby!) for a photo keepsake you'll all marvel over within a few months. While many hospitals still provide footprints of a baby at birth, a photo showing family foot size comparisons is even more special! Another option is to line up family shoes for a photo that contrasts differences in size.

Jingle bell anklet

Tie a jingle bell or two onto an elastic, tie it into a loop that will fit gently around your infant's ankle, then place it on baby's ankle and cover securely with a sock (to prevent any possibility of the bell being pulled off or ingested). Baby will love kicking her feet to hear the bells.

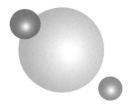

Wreath of life

This is such an easy activity to do with your baby, and the result is a keepsake you will treasure forever! On each month's anniversary of your baby's birth, create a handprint on card stock using safe, washable paint. (You create your own color scheme.) When baby turns one year old, connect each handprint together with a ribbon and glue as needed to create a circular wreath shape. Don't worry about handprints being perfect; it's part of the charm. Finish the wreath with a big bow, and consider dangling a favorite photo of your baby in the middle of the wreath with ribbon. This also makes a great gift for grandparents!

2

A Star Is Born

Games and activities for
3 to 6 months

There's no shortage of family fun when imagination, activity, and role playing are added to the mix!

Your precious infant's personality is starting to emerge, and most likely she is beginning to love being the star attraction!

Whether it's an enthusiastic waving of the arms or kicking of the feet, most infants at about this stage are unmistakably excited when seeing loved ones, toys, or even anticipating a beloved activity (like a bath), and won't hesitate to let you know. This is a great time during a baby's first year for introducing some physical interactions and stimulations.

At six months, your infant has transitioned into a burgeoning baby, who day by day is becoming more alert and undoubtedly more mobile. Muscle control is strengthening, and many babies will be rolling over from back to stomach and may begin to push themselves and their previously wobbly head up, to see the world more clearly.

Seeing

Jack in the box

Your baby will delight in a jack-in-the-box style game, and you don't need to buy a toy to have fun with this concept. You can create the same surprise by simply cutting a hole out of the bottom of a small box and putting a glove or finger puppet on your hand. Sing a silly song or simply ask your baby to watch what pops out and then spring out your hand! Your baby is beginning to understand the concept of object permanence, which will make this game especially exciting.

Objects afar

Your baby's sight has now developed to the point that she can see in color and has a defined sense of depth perception. Try to place coveted objects across the room and watch whether she can find them. Show your baby a colorful toy or stuffed animal, place it at a distance, and see whether she looks for it. Watch her reaction when she locates it!

To encourage baby's perception of colors, put brightly-colored and different socks on her feet and draw attention to them. Wiggle the ends of the socks and ask your baby, "Where are your toes? What color are your socks?"

Day and night

Put some sunglasses on your baby and take him out for a spin outdoors. Tell him he is one "cool dude." Sunglasses will protect baby's eyes, so you can get him used to wearing them at an early age so he won't resist later!

Then take your baby outside on a bright, star-filled night and let him admire the stars. Weather permitting, lay out a blanket and just stargaze quietly. You will enjoy spending this time with your baby in a fun setting even more than looking at the sky!

A New View

This is a great stage to carry baby with her head above your shoulder, so she can get a new view of the world. Walk around indoors and out, letting her look backward over your shoulder for some interesting new perspectives.

Sinking ship

Use bath time fun to show your baby that objects are still there even if he can't see them. Show him a plastic ship (or something similar) and then have it sink under water. Ask baby, "Where is the ship?" Then bring the ship back up to the top of the water. Repeat again. Let baby try it himself.

Hi, friend!

Your baby is still too young to have friends or even to understand the concept of playing with others. But that won't stop him from enjoying looking at another baby and watching how he moves and sounds. This is a good age to begin introducing him to other babies on play dates or through child care.

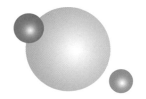

Who's that baby?

Show your baby his beautiful image in the mirror. Say, "Who's that baby? That's you. That is (baby's name)!" Find a small mirror he can hold (with adult support and supervision) and let him look at himself. Or even better, purchase a baby-friendly mirror toy he can take with him and use to gaze at himself whenever he likes!

Designer in training

Your baby is now interested in finer details, so show her things she never noticed before, such as intricate details on toys, the pattern on his room's wallpaper, or even the eyes, nose, and mouth of his favorite stuffed animal. Many babies find the details utterly fascinating at this stage.

Flashlight fun

Your baby is now old enough to enjoy a light show with a flashlight. Lie on your bed with baby, turn off the lights, and you can have a flashlight performance involving whirls of light. Turn the flashlight on and off, spotlight different objects in the room, and just be silly. Mom and dad can share a light show for extra entertainment.

Tree watch

Lay with your infant under a big tree and let her watch how the leaves move in the breeze and how the sunlight glistens through the branches.

To market, to market

As soon as your baby can sit upright without bobbles, the new world of riding in a shopping cart awaits. Find a stress-free, leisurely time to stroll through grocery aisles and introduce baby to different types of food, merchandise, and even smells! You can encourage name association by saying things like, "See the red apples?"

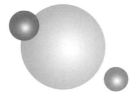

Hearing

ABCs

Some parents struggle with songs to sing to their baby without feeling silly, but a good one to sing throughout a baby's first few years is the "ABC" song. Your baby will be interested in watching your features as you sing it, and the consistency of you singing it with every diaper change or at set intervals will truly help her later when it's time to learn those letters. (But right now, of course, all she'll do is crave your voice!) You can also start adding words that begin with each letter as a way to emphasize talking out loud to your baby, such as "D is for diaper" or "B is for bath time!"

Smack and blow kiss

Start a ritual of a loud smack-and-blow kiss as you say hello and good-bye to your baby, and before long she will be reciprocating. Your infant will also associate the smack sound with a loving feeling.

Coyote howl

Your baby won't understand why you're howling at the moon, but will find your silliness hysterical. Take your tot out on a full moon evening, show him the big full moon, and then let out a coyote-sized howl.

Good Morning, Pumpkin

Don't be afraid to call your "lil' pumpkin" some pet nickname or term of endearment. If you greet him with your own silly or sweet name when you wake him up each morning, for example, it becomes part of his routine that he will look forward to. Most parents have a sweet nickname for their baby, so don't be afraid to say it out loud. Or, if you prefer, keep it as a special secret between the two of you. Just don't forget to record the sentiment in baby's book for the future!

Gum pop

Blow some really big bubbles for baby and then let them pop! He'll find the noise and the big bubble-face funny!

Pots and pans band

Although you won't want this activity all the time, go ahead and bring out your pots and pans and let baby bang the lid on pans just so he can hear the result. Babies love the "big bang" action!

Rattles

Rattles have remained a popular baby toy throughout time, and with good reason. Rattles provide something to clench, they make noise, and they provide stimulation and reinforcement for a baby (the more a baby shakes, the more it makes sound). Wrist rattles are a great stimulation for many babies, but watch your child's cues carefully to make sure he doesn't grow frustrated over wanting the rattle off or wanting it to stop making noise, which often results in flailing (and more noise!).

Diaper jungle

As baby becomes more active, diaper changes become a greater challenge. Create a jungle of animal sound effects each time you change baby's diaper . . . one time you're a mighty lion, the next a monkey, and then an elephant. Be silly and exaggerated with your noises—at least long enough to get the mission accomplished!

Not Too Close, Not Too Far

Babies need time on their own when awake, but will do best when they hear a loved one nearby. Look for times when you can safely place baby on a blanket with toys and encourage independent play while you are nearby but not directly interacting (such as folding clothes in the same room, for example). Talk aloud and let your baby know you are near. As baby develops, she will be able to amuse herself for longer periods of time, but try to come back to her before she starts to fuss to keep it a positive experience.

Tickle bee

Buzz like a bee and move your fingers around like a bee flying through the air. Then swoop down and land on baby's tummy, head, arm, or leg, and fly back off again. Your baby will love following the buzzing sound and watching your fingers for the next landing spot.

Baby's name

Your baby can now recognize and respond to her own name. This is a case in which name calling should be encouraged! Make it a habit to say her name as often as possible and get a reaction.

Touch

Spoon and spatula

Give your baby a small wooden spoon and a spatula, and let her touch and feel their various textures. Note how she reacts to the wooden part (some find it interesting; some do not like the feeling at all). The rubber part of the spatula can be fun to play with, and some stores have mini versions that are perfect for baby's hands.

Snuggle bunnies

Find some particularly snuggly stuffed animals and encourage your infant to feel their texture and learn to "hug" or love them. Some animals feature different textures that babies may find intriguing.

It's often used as a term of endearment, but it's at this stage that many babies truly become "snuggle bunnies" with a favorite stuffed animal, toy, or even favorite person. Babies love to hug and snuggle with something (or someone) familiar. Often, babies will take to a certain item that they rely on for emotional comfort and soothing. If it's *you* that your baby prefers, be sure to offer up a lot of snuggle bunny time and teach the art of snuggling and hugging. Before long, your baby will be too busy to want to snuggle as much.

Dad's stubble

Let your baby explore some new textures, such as dad's facial stubble or facial hair. Facial stubble is a texture that many infants find quite interesting. Dad can make a ritual out of letting baby touch his stubble or facial hair, and then his smooth face (if he shaves).

How much love?

Play the "How Much Do I Love You?" game by telling your baby how much you love him using lots of enthusiasm and hugs. Extend your arms as far outward as possible, as high as you can, as low as you can go, and then wrap those loving arms around him and give him a nice bear hug. Your baby will love the attention and the mighty big hugs.

Toilet paper time

Let your baby play with a small roll of toilet paper (under close supervision). Let her unroll it, tear it, wrap it, throw it (just not eat it). Your baby will find unrolling it and just feeling its texture a fascinating activity!

Nap nuzzles

Transform your body into a lap pillow, and allow your child to take a nap on your tummy while you enjoy some unabashed quality nuzzling time. Parents often yearn for quiet moments spent just listening to baby's sweet slumber and sighs, and it's a perfect opportunity to get in those long gazes and snuggles that are often hard to come by when everyone is on the go. Just snuggling up feels as good for mom or dad as it does for baby.

Tactile touch

Give your baby some tactile stimulation by letting him feel the different textured objects you have around the house. Or, weather permitting, head outdoors! Have your baby feel different objects and simply describe them while touching. Experiment with soft satiny fabrics, rough items such as tree bark, and fluffy objects such as cotton balls.

Taste and smell

Family mealtime

Now is the time to start making your baby feel part of the family during mealtime. If you haven't already done so, go ahead and set up that high chair. Baby's only source of nutrition may still be a bottle, but set her feeding schedule to coincide with family meals. She will enjoy the family interaction and will smell and see foods that will be in her near future.

What's that smell?

Baby has a good sense of smell, and while she isn't eating much at this stage, her curiosity for scents is growing constantly. Let your baby experience the more interesting smells around her, such as the scent of your chewing gum, your cologne, how it smells outdoors after a rain, the aroma of popcorn, or even the smell of your pet's food.

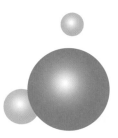

Book bites

Babies will want to explore books by "tasting" them because they don't yet understand their purpose. Keep your baby books clean and go ahead and let baby "taste" a book. Continue to read to your baby regularly; he will eventually outgrow this desire to "taste" curious objects such as books.

Food fest

Baby is now ready to start eating solid foods, and you can make your own baby food inexpensively and conveniently. Select fresh produce, wash appropriately, boil until tender, and puree in a food processor or blender, and then scoop portions into an ice-cube tray for easy storage. Once frozen, store each cube in a small plastic baggie, labeled with the date. Remember that babies do not need any seasoning; they have better taste buds than you do.

Let your baby practice feeding herself with her own child-friendly spoon and small bowl. Most babies like to taste, and even lick, a spoon for the experience. You can encourage "pretend play" at this stage; it won't be long before she starts demanding real food!

If the doctor agrees, give your baby a snack of cheerios or similar type of "Os" cereal. Baby can scoop them into her hand with a simple motion, which promotes self-feeding.

Language development

Hello teacher

This stage is an ideal time to "teach" your child about your life and her family. Of course, baby won't really internalize or remember the details you are saying yet, but will love to hear your words. Start talking about things you want for her, hopes and dreams, family history, etc. Tell your baby you're her first teacher and that you'll be there to help her along the way. Every time she coos or babbles, reinforce her early language skills with high praise.

The Crowd Pleaser

Show your infant how to bestow exaggerated kiss smacks. Everyone will be charmed!

It's for you, baby!

Go ahead, let baby listen to someone talking to her on the telephone. She can enjoy conversations with grandparents or mom or dad on the phone, and may even gurgle or coo in response to certain voices! You can also let her listen in when you play your voice messages as another way to gain familiarity with voices and speech patterns.

Squeal off

Have a silly "squeal off" contest with your baby. Let your inhibitions go and make the goofiest squeals and exaggerated gestures possible. Encourage your baby to mimic the squeals back! You can "squeal" with delight at interesting objects or just with joy at seeing your precious one!

Baaaa beats and rhythms

Your baby is beginning to understand the rhythm of speech. Talk to your baby and then wait for a response. She'll begin to "talk" back and then wait for you to respond again. This is the beginning of an early conversation!

She is also making "baa" sounds now, so show her how to mimic back with some rhythm. Instead of words, do some baaa-beats, and encourage her to create some of her own.

Up and down

Have an up-and-down playtime experience with baby. Each time you pick him up, say "up" and then likewise with "down." Swoosh him up and then slowly go down, and then go for other variations. Baby will soon learn this spatial concept and "up" is an early word many babies speak.

Simple signs

Crawling is to walking as signing is to talking, according to experts, and no formal education is needed to bring sign language into early communications with baby. You can pick up a book on the topic or go on the Internet to learn basic sign language symbols, and then use them with your baby while you also say aloud the words you are signing.

Proponents of baby sign language say that most babies can begin signing words before they can communicate them orally. Begin with two or three signs that are most valuable to you and baby, such as *eat*, *sleep*, and *stop*.

Baby's First Language

Your baby is fine-tuning his cries to get the reaction he wants. He has developed different cries for different needs, and now it's up to you to figure out the meanings!

Motor development

Crib gyms

Find an inexpensive crib gym toy that promotes motor skill development and encourages your baby to bat and kick objects while lying on her back. To help get her started, try dangling a favorite toy or colorful animal above her crib and entice her to "get it." You can also hold a line of toys (such as plastic connectible objects that are safe for baby) over your infant's head and encourage her to reach for them.

Turtle dance

While on their tummies, babies may "swim" or do a turtle dance at this stage, which is nothing more than precious preliminary movements to prepare for crawling. Be sure to give baby ample floor time to work those arms and legs.

Bye-bye

Show your baby how to wave bye-bye to loved ones. At this stage, your baby will be developing the coordination to enchant everyone with a sweet wave (with parent's help, of course)!

Flap and fly

Encourage your baby to flap his arms like a bird. Have one adult lift and lower baby while holding onto his waist and have the other adult mimic his arm moves. It's a great motor development exercise and he will love soaring like a bird! Be sure to add some bird chirps for effect!

When he's ready to take flight, hoist your baby safely into the air (with your hands grasping him on both sides) and tell him to fly before bringing him down for a landing. Tell him "shoo fly!" and then pick him up and sail to another location.

Hand off

Play hand off games that will encourage your baby to grasp and hold onto objects. Give your baby something to hold, and then ask him to give it back to you.

Or try giving him one item, and then while he is holding onto it, hand him another and then even a third object, and see how he chooses which ones to hold and look over!

As a variation, show baby how to stack things up and then knock them down. Hand baby one item after another and teach him how to stack them up. Empty individual-sized cereal boxes work well. This fun play helps promote the development of baby's grasp.

The Dropping Game

It's inevitable that babies like to drop things like bottles, cups, spoons, or toys from their high chair, stroller, swing, etc., mainly because they love to watch someone retrieve it just so they can do it again. While at times frustrating, parents should realize that it really is a learning experience for babies; they are not intentionally trying to annoy you!

Fun on the floor

Your baby's neck muscles should be strong enough for him to do mini push-ups by raising his chest and head off the floor while on his tummy. Encourage him to continue pushing himself up to further strengthen muscles, and while you're at it, why not do the same yourself!

Many babies scoot along on their bottoms as an early form of transportation. Make it a game of rootin'-tootin' scooting fun along the floor with you by baby's side. If your tot doesn't scoot, then hold him against your bent legs and scoot on the floor. This will be fun for you both.

One of the best ways to get baby active on the floor is scatter toys around so that he can move from one object to another independently. Encourage your baby to choose and "do" versus just watching! Note what your baby seems to choose as favorites.

To get really silly, stuff a long sock (such as a white athletic tube sock), close up the end with needle and thread or even a tie fastener, and pretend it's a snake. Slither it on the floor or up near baby (making sure to keep it funny and not scary) and make silly snake noises!

Bed bounce

Go ahead and let your baby bounce on your bed (with adult support, of course)! While holding onto baby's waist, encourage her to jump up and down on your bed to strengthen those leg muscles and encourage body control. Never let your baby get on your bed without an adult.

Creeping along

Your baby is starting to find inventive ways to wiggle, drag, scoot, or propel while on her tummy. Help your baby maneuver early transportation moves by placing her on her tummy and moving her legs back and forth. You can also work with your baby on "reach and pull" movements with her arms.

For a fun way to encourage your baby to get up on all four limbs, show her how to wag her bottom like a tail (you'll need to demonstrate, of course!). She may tip over so make sure there is nothing to bump into nearby.

Push 'n' pull

Babies at this stage are becoming interested in cause and effect. Play object games such as push and pull so baby can see what happens to a toy if she pushes it over the edge of a table. What occurs if baby is pushing and you are pulling? Have fun with this type of developmental play.

Sitting pretty

Most babies can now pull themselves to a sitting position and sit upright with supports. Plan family time together by telling baby you're going to read to her on the couch and establish a pattern of her sitting there with mom and dad (adult supervision always is required). Sit on either side of your baby and share books or play simple baby games or activities, or even watch a TV show together as family.

Encouraging Head Turns

Parents can roll a ball to each other across the floor while baby is watching to encourage her to turn her head and follow the action.

Hand to hand

Your baby can now transfer objects from hand to hand, and fist-sized balls (ones that are too big for the mouth) can provide lots of fun. Cat ball toys with a bell inside provide special charm for babies and are often the right size; plastic rings are also fun. If your baby is not already doing this on her own, help her learn by showing her how to do it. Another way is to offer something she wants to the hand that is already holding something, and see whether she will transfer the object.

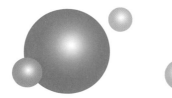

Family fun

Blast off!

If your baby's neck muscles are well developed at this age (if not, wait until they are), you can enjoy a fun game of "blast off!" Lie on your back and place your baby's face down on your chest. Count "3-2-1" and then "blast off!" by raising your baby into the air. You can take your baby on a brief flight before landing back on your chest.

Ride the horsey

Have one lucky adult bend down on all fours. Then, have a second adult hold baby securely around the waist and rest her on the back of the "horsey." While holding baby securely in place, take her for a horseback ride! She will think this is absolutely hilarious!

Stomach crunches (yours)

You can exercise your stomach by doing crunches, baby-style, by lying on your back and holding baby propped up on your bent knees. While holding onto baby, lie back and then bring your body up, while keeping stomach muscles tight. Repeat as you can. Baby will like the interaction, and you'll like the results!

Where's Baby?

Use a small hand towel or burp rag and place it in front of baby's face and say, "Where's baby?" Pull it off, and then exclaim, "There she is!" Babies love this game, often for several months of their first year!

Baby bubble bath

Use a small amount of child-friendly bubble bath in a small container and create some foam that your baby can play with safely. Your youngster is developing a sense of humor, and may find the feel and silliness of bubbles hilarious! You'll be sure to please if you make a bubble mustache or bubble hair on yourself and model for baby!

House helper

No one ever said cleaning house is fun, but make it a game with baby by doing pick-up tasks in his room in the morning or after naps while he's still in his crib. He'll love watching you around his room and observing you squirting, wiping, cleaning, and even vacuuming from a safe distance. You can count diapers as you restock, sing while you dust, and even dance around the room as you pick up toys and items.

Making sure baby stays safe, let him go for a ride in the laundry basket as you carry clothes from hampers to the washer. He'll think it is great fun, and it's a way to watch baby and do chores at the same time!

Baby Loves to Hear Your Voice

At about three months, your newborn will turn his head to follow a sound. So it's particularly important at this stage to verbalize all the time. Use your voice to let baby know where mom and dad are and what they're doing!

Baby weight

What better way to tone up after baby than by using your baby as weights? It's a fun activity for mom or dad, and your baby will enjoy the attention! To work on your arms, you can hold your infant facing you with your hands on either side of his waist and then slowly extend your arms out straight and then bring him back close to you. While on your back, you can place him safely on your stomach and practice mini crunches or leg lifts.

Goodnight, baby

Create a special family ritual for putting baby to bed (just be sure it's something that you can live with). Whether it's a piggyback ride, a bedtime book, a back massage, or sweet lullaby, your baby is now at the stage where he craves certain consistencies with his life. Establish a routine now that will carry you through the toddler years!

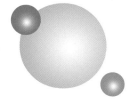

Balloon watch

Many babies at this stage like to watch colorful balloons, and parents can try tying a balloon on a baby's stroller so that baby can view its movement. Watch baby closely however, to ensure the balloon doesn't agitate her, or worse, that she gets it and either squeezes it or tries to bite on it, often with a terrifying (to baby) result!

Peek-a-boo

Classic baby games continue to be popular because they're foolproof! Don't overlook the ever-favorite peek-a-boo. Cover your face with your hands or a kerchief, then remove and exclaim, "Peek-a-boo. I see you!" As baby develops, leave your baby's sight for a few seconds, and then pop back in again. This helps baby to know that you may be out of sight, but you are still present!

Leg ups

While sitting on the floor or a chair with your legs out in front, lay your infant on one leg in a stomach-to-leg position, and while holding on, lift baby up and down while bending your knees. If you want to add extra fun, play some child-friendly music and lift and lower with the beat.

Silly exclamations

Play the classic "This little piggy went to a market" game with baby's toes. Really build up the "wee-wee-wee, all the way home" portion. It's sure to get a squeal!

Or give a great big smile, open your eyes big, and tell your baby, "I'm gonna kiss your tummy!" Then, "I'm gonna kiss your toes!" and so on. This early fun introduces first associations with parts of the body.

Lovingly tweak your baby's nose, and say "I've got your nose!" Remember, it's really the inflection of your voice that babies respond to versus what you say at this age.

Arts and crafts

Baby bling

Add some trendy "baby bling" to a simple canvas bag by affixing rhinestones, crystals, and glitter fabric paint to create a one-of-a-kind diaper bag style statement. Trace baby's handprints on a sheet of paper and then use it as a guide to transfer it over to the tote. If you're really creative, take some photos of baby and the family, print the photos off on transfer paper, iron them on as desired, and then add sparkly details. Some fun looks include pirates or adventure heroes on items for boys and diva or princess styles for girls.

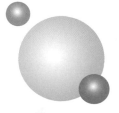

Milk jug juggles

Clean out empty plastic milk jugs and give them to baby to grasp and clang together. Consider cutting the opening bigger and show baby how to put safe objects into the jug and take them out!

Paper plate faces

Create some baby-friendly masks with paper plates. Using an inexpensive paper plate, cut out eyes (and other features, if desired) and decorate it as whatever character is desired. It can be a princess, a pirate, a silly face, an animal, or even an icon such as a silly smiley face. Glue a Popsicle stick to the bottom to create a handle and entertain baby with your many silly faces!

Greetings to you!

Recycle colorful greeting cards by tucking them around baby's changing table area and letting her grab and look at them while being changed.

Sponge stamps

Purchase some inexpensive sponges (those without scrubber material on one side) and cut them into simple shapes, such as a fish, star, circle, square, or triangle. Wet the sponges slightly and let your baby make water stamp prints on the patio or driveway.

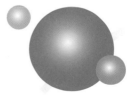

Adventure World
Games and activities for
6 to 9 months

The world is getting a little bigger and your baby is ready to explore. All sights and sounds are new, and every day is a grand adventure!

3

Your baby may seem to be everywhere and into every-thing, all at once. Increased maneuverability means additional freedom as well as new safety concerns.

Parents often feel pulled between delighting in their baby's newfound skills and the fatigue from having to move everything and watch out for potentially harmful things. Now is the time to work on your baby's new motor skills with activities for reaching, grasping, pushing, and body control.

By the nine-month mark, some teeth are in, and your baby is growing phenomenally in both size and develop-ment. He is adept at handling solid foods, is more intent on listening, is beginning to initiate conversations, and most likely, doesn't want to be separated from mom and dad for too long.

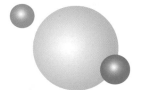

Seeing

Light on, light off

Babies find about every single thing intriguing at this stage—after all, that's how they learn. Pique your baby's interest in cause and effect by letting him turn a light switch on and off and then see what happens. In fact, encourage *him* to be the one to turn on a switch as you enter a room and turn it off when you leave. You're starting some energy-saving habits early!

Body Exploration is Normal at this Stage

Your baby will focus on his various body parts by exploring with his mouth and hands and acutely viewing fingers, toes, belly button, and even genitals. Support your baby's exploration and clearly identify the names of various body parts, and encourage your baby to touch his toes, feel his hair, tug his ear, etc.

Plastic bottle pretend

Shampoo bottles come in an array of colors, shapes, and designs. Instead of throwing empty ones away, let your baby pretend to shampoo his hair or just look at the colors of the bottles. Show him how you can see through certain bottles. You may find he prefers these plastic toys over some of his more pricey items!

Pattern patrol

Boost your baby's emerging interest in details by showing him contrasting geometric designs and colorful patterns. Many books showcase intricate patterns and shapes; you can also let baby sit on your lap at the computer and locate some of these patterns for viewing on the Internet. You'll be amazed at how your baby can concentrate now on objects he finds interesting!

Shy away

Babies at this stage begin to be shy with people they don't know. You can help lessen stranger aversion by encouraging social contacts while you are still present. Talk with your baby about the details of someone she is meeting ("See Aunt Ann's blue dress? Isn't it pretty?"). Above all, understand that this is a normal reaction and that your baby will outgrow the shyness around individuals he doesn't know well.

See-through fun

Let your baby play with some clear plasticware, such as plates and cups that she can peer through. Baby will like sticking her hand in a cup while still being able to view her fingers, for example, and will find the notion of "see through" fascinating.

Outdoor peek-a-boo

Your baby loves games in which she peeks and hides, so show her how to peer through bushes outdoors by separating branches and peeking through at something . . . or someone! She'll think she is invisible! If you don't have a safe location outdoors, you can play the same game by peering through clothes in a closet.

New Skills and Understanding

Your baby understands the purpose of an increasing number of objects, and is perhaps even reaching out for things. If you tell your baby it's time for bath, for example, he may reach out for the bathtub or even some favorite bath toys. Encourage his growing skills of association and purpose.

Red, yellow, green

Draw your baby's attention to the traffic lights while in the car. Describe the color of the signal and point out how it changes to another color. It's a great way to teach baby these three basic colors!

Funny reflection

Place silly hats, headbands, or even small, soft toys (such as a small stuffed animal) on baby's head and then let her look at herself in the mirror. Encourage her to take it off and look at it. Then, lower baby away from the mirror, place something else on her head and pop up for a surprise! This is a fun game as baby's focus and self-awareness improves!

Object games

Your baby continues to strengthen his focus and interest in objects and people, and is starting to develop a rudimentary sense of "place." Move an object totally out of place and see whether your baby notices and has any reaction as a result. It can be a shoe placed in the pet's bed, a sock on mom's head, or a piece of crumbled paper on baby's highchair tray.

Or, place a small object under one of two bowls (placed upside down) and have your baby guess and lift to see which bowl the item is under. Move the bowls around and then let him choose and lift again. Some babies at this stage will be able to put an object underneath and surprise mom or dad as well!

You can gauge baby's preferences (at least for that very moment) by engaging him in a simple game of pick and choose. Place two objects in front of your baby and ask him to choose one. See which one he prefers (and don't be upset if he double-reaches and grabs both). Make it a game by giving options; soon, he'll understand that he does have this decision-making ability.

Hearing

An earful for baby

Give your baby an earful . . . of noises, that is, by sharing with him the many different sounds he can hear in the car. Because most babies spend some time on the go, your baby is now in tune enough to listen to things such as the car radio, air-conditioning, horn, windshield wipers, and even a car window raising and lowering. Talk about each of the different sounds with your baby and associate words with the sounds for early language development.

Hands up game

Find a squeaky toy or bell and show your baby how to play "hands up." Show your baby how to raise his arms (or another gesture of your choosing) whenever he hears a certain sound, and turn it into a fun game. (This activity also allows you to observe hearing awareness.) Let baby then have a try at making the sound himself, while you be the one to respond.

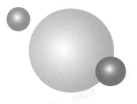

Shake up!

Your baby will love to shake things, sometimes almost seeming to frenzy over the activity. Find some objects or toys that baby can safely shake while he listens to the sounds the movement makes.

Simple (and Noisy) Fun

Two wooden blocks banged together can create a lot of noise . . . and fun for baby! Join in with your own set, and you can create a block symphony!

Applause, applause!

Teach your baby how to clap! Clapping is a fairly simple skill and your baby will enjoy learning about the cause and effect of the motion—that bringing her hands together will result in a large "clap" sound. You can also show her when clapping is appropriate by clapping for her when she achieves something new!

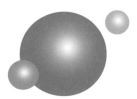

Body sounds

Your baby is becoming interested in the sounds that bodies make. Let her listen to your heartbeat or pounding pulse after rigorous activity, the sound of your stomach growling, hiccups, yawns, and even belches (say "excuse me," of course!).

Pen clicker

You know the sometimes-annoying sound of the constant clicking of a pen? Many babies will like the rhythmic clicking sound you can make by clicking it open and then closed. The sound is a way to hold baby's attention (or divert) on a short-term basis!

Early Empathy in Babies

Have you noticed how when one baby cries, another joins in? This is early empathy building, and your baby is starting to cue in to others' emotions and needs.

Shoe dance

Give your baby a pair of her shoes, grab a pair for yourself, and show her how to have a shoe dance by tapping them on the floor. Make clackety-clack, popping, or sliding motions on tile or any hard surface.

Bell song

Use a small bell to catch baby's attention. The tone is pleasant to the ear and you can simply jingle it when you want her attention. Because your baby's focus will shift quickly, use a small bell as a pleasant way to talk with her and to pique her interest on something to look at or to participate in. (Just remember: baby should not be allowed to play with the bell because its ringer could detach and become a choking hazard.)

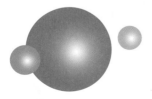

Musical pop-up fun

Musical pop-up toys are particularly fun at this stage, because your baby has learned or is learning all about cause-and-effect. Find a toy that baby can successfully self-activate, complete with music for extra fun.

Is that my name?

Your baby should know and respond to his name by now, but saying it various ways helps to expand his scope of name recognition. Call your baby's name in different tones and sing-song voices and encourage a response. Sound it out slowly, repeat it rapidly, and make it a name-calling game. Challenge baby to learn all the variations of this all-important word!

Touch

Face fun

Let your baby explore your face by placing his hand on different parts: ear, eye, nose, chin, etc. As he touches each part, say aloud what it is. Let him touch your nose and then you touch his. Get up close and personal with your baby and bestow some eyelash kisses on his cheek. Simply flutter your eyes up and down rapidly!

Reach out and pat

Babies at this stage like to "pat" things . . . whether it's you, other kids, pets, or objects. Encourage this gesture as it is a way of active exploration and an opportunity to feel things. Provide some interesting objects for baby to pat, but be sure to have him supervised when touching animals and other kids, so as not to accidentally hurt them.

Rub a dub

Your baby is now independent enough to apply soap to her body (or at least try) during bath time. Give baby a soft sponge with baby soap already applied and let her try to soap her body and wash herself. She'll think it's great fun, and some soap may even end up in the right places!

For added fun and motor skill development, purchase some rubber squirt toys and show your baby how to use them in the bathtub. A sport-style water bottle also works well and is easy for little hands to grasp.

Start a Good Habit Now

Even if your baby only has a couple of teeth, introduce her to a baby toothbrush and let her experience what a toothbrush feels like. Do not use toothpaste on baby unless directed by a pediatrician; water will work well at this stage.

Target practice

Place your hands down by baby's feet, and encourage a friendly game of target practice. Encourage baby to kick your hands (the target), and make a dinging noise every time he makes contact.

Plastic hanger duel

Let your baby explore through touch and even taste a clean baby-size plastic clothes hanger (many babies find their shape and indentations interesting). Your baby may also enjoy a friendly game of "hanger duel" in which you each hold a hanger and clank it onto the other, as if having a friendly duel.

Rock 'n' roll

Find some small rocks (not too small) and let your baby touch and feel their texture. Let her put them in a bucket and take them out again. Closely supervise her handling of the rocks, making sure they don't end up in her mouth.

Kitchen playground

Your kitchen is a great resource for simple activities that baby is sure to find entertaining! Give baby **a wooden spoon and bowl**, and let her practice stirring. If you dare, add something she can stir, such as water, a small amount of baby food, even pudding. (Be prepared for a mess!) Baby will like the sensation of stirring and mixing.

Or, give baby **two wooden spoons** she can use to pound on a plate, a pan, a metal object, or a similar object. Babies have natural rhythm; go ahead and enjoy the melody!

Use a **cookie sheet** to let your baby play with child-friendly magnets, such as alphabet or animal shapes. (Be sure to closely supervise your baby to make sure no objects are put into her mouth.) Your baby will like putting on and taking off the magnet shapes.

Muffin tins are a great baby toy because babies can sort and stack things inside the tins. Even muffin paper liners can provide baby with fun by showing her how to place one in each tin. Add a paper cup, a ball, or whatever she likes.

Put **plastic bowls** on your head, and baby's too, and be silly bowl heads. Your baby may like taking it off and then trying to put it back on himself. Or let your baby play with some **plastic cups**, and show him how to stack them or turn them over and build a small pyramid. Of course, the fun is in knocking them down!

Hair rinse

If your baby is comfortable in the bathtub, let him have a try at rinsing his hair after a shampoo (or just wetting it). Give him a cup of water when he's in the tub, and show him how to pour it over his head. Most babies like the sensation of running water over their heads, especially when they're the ones to cause it!

Hot and cold

Compare and contrast temperature in ways that baby can begin to relate to. While keeping the temperatures safe, let him feel warm water and then cold water, or let him feel the outside of your warm coffee cup compared with an iced drink. You can give him a cold Popsicle and then contrast it with food that is warm. Say the words "warm" and "cold" along with each sensation, to help encourage early word association.

Lotion rub

Squirt a small amount of baby lotion into your tot's hands, and show him how to rub it on his body for soft, smooth skin. Many babies prefer to rub lotion on others, so encourage the "favor" and be sure to offer lots of praise!

Spray bottle fun

Your baby should be able to operate a simple spray bottle (find one that is easy to use). Fill it with water and on a warm day take your baby outside and let him squirt water at things. Watch out, you could be the target! Baby-friendly spray bottles can also be used in the bathtub.

Squishy play

Put something squishy, such as apple sauce, inside a sealed Ziploc bag and let your baby squeeze and play with it (under your direct supervision). This is a mess-free way to let baby experience some new textures, and the squishy sensation can be a lot of fun! As with anything plastic, be sure baby doesn't place the baggie over her nose or mouth.

Taste and smell

Breath alert

Let your baby smell your breath after you've just brushed your teeth, are chewing gum, or have just eaten an interesting food. Don't forget that baby is quite curious and has a well-developed sense of smell, so he shouldn't mind discovering a whiff of your breath (as long as it's not too unpleasant)!

Smelling lesson

Take your baby on a scent walk indoors and out, and show him how to actively "sniff" something such as a flower or even a food item. Teach him to use his sense of smell, and to respond with an understanding when his "nose knows" something! ("I smell dinner cooking. Do you smell that chicken? Doesn't it smell yummy?")

Backyard picnic

Throw down a blanket in the backyard (or park setting) and have a simple picnic with your baby. Bring along a packed picnic basket with baby-appropriate eats and drinks, and spend time outdoors. If weather isn't appropriate, then have an indoor picnic in your living room. Your baby will enjoy the ritual of a picnic and like having a chance to eat and play in a different setting.

Movie night

Have a special in-home movie outing with your baby. Spread out a blanket in front of the television, give your baby an approved finger-food snack (such as cut-up grapes, a banana, or Cheerios, for example) and watch a kid movie together. Some families have a monthly movie night as a family experience, and there is no reason baby can't join right in!

Fun shapes

Be creative with your food presentations with baby by occasionally turning his carrot chunks into a flower design or any other interesting appearance. Go ahead and make a smiley face on his piece of sandwich bread or make a smiley face using grapes cut in half. It's a good way to encourage his interest in different types of food.

Finger food adventures

Have a stacking contest with Cheerios or other "o"-shaped cereal and pretend you're swimming with Goldfish snacks at the bottom of the sea. These finger food adventures should take place somewhere other than where baby eats, such as the park or at an activity table, to avoid giving baby the idea (more than he will already have) of "playing" with his food.

For a fun activity that is dinner table appropriate, share a banana with baby. Peel a banana and give baby a bite, and then have him give you a bite back (substitute with another food if bananas are not okay for your baby's diet). This simple gesture lets baby learn to care for others and teaches early sharing!

Let's Brush Together

While some infants may start getting teeth earlier than six months, this is the average time that those first baby teeth make their debut. Begin brushing your baby's teeth as soon as they come in with a special soft infant toothbrush and water or non-fluoridated training toothpaste (check with your pediatric dentist). Turn it into family fun by having everyone have a tooth-brushing ritual every morning and evening together!

Language development

First expressions

Encourage early expression words such as "ma-ma-ma" and "da-da-da" by asking your baby to use his voice whenever he wants something. Provide positive reinforcement whenever he attempts to make these sounds, and ask him to use his words for expression. Of course, language is still undeveloped at this time, but it's a good stage to start!

Tell your baby out loud how much you love him, and encourage him to vocalize the affection back. Encourage him to also vocalize and show his love toward a favorite stuffed animal or toy.

Bounce off

Bounce baby on your legs while changing your voice pitch with each number and say, "One, two, three, and four. Baby wants to bounce some more. Four, three, two, one. Baby wants to have some fun!" Your baby will like the silly rhyme in conjunction with the bouncing motion.

High chair musical

Make the transition to a high chair a fun, positive milestone. After baby is placed in her high chair and while you're preparing the meal, create a tradition of singing to your youngster and encourage her to croon in return. You can make up silly songs about the food she's about to eat.

Routine adjustments

At this age and stage, your baby might start to squawk about getting dressed or getting her diaper changed. So, stir up the mix and create some routine adjustments. After all, who said babies always have to get a diaper change at their changing table or get dressed in the bedroom? Find some fun new ways to avoid monotony for baby while keeping it convenient for you.

Alphabet starters

Take a letter of the alphabet each day and sing-song it to baby. For example, "A-aa-aa-a; that's the sound A makes. Baby, can you say A-aa-aa-a?" It's never too early to start vocalizing the sounds of the alphabet and encouraging baby to repeat them back. Your baby, as brilliant as he is, won't relate the sounds to the actual letters yet, but it's a fun vocalization exercise and baby is sure to delight in the sound of your voice.

Sound effects

Encourage your baby to make the sound effects associated with an object (for example, the puttering sound for a boat or the ringing sound for a telephone). Mimicking sounds is a common milestone at this stage, so be sure to get your lips sputtering with plenty of special noises and effects that baby can copy.

Motor development

Bundle of motion

Your baby will likely learn to bounce up and down on his legs while upright, which is a great leg strengthening exercise and precursor to walking. Encourage baby to bounce by providing safe and sturdy waist-high objects for him to hold onto.

During this stage, he will learn to shake his head "no" soon enough, but for now, enjoy the head shakes by turning them into a game. Have baby shake his head "no" from side to side and then "yes" up and down. Then, do a head shake frenzy all around for fun!

And if your baby begins to rise to his hands and knees, rock back and forth, reach out tentatively . . . you've got a crawler! Some babies may need some prompting, so don't be afraid to get on your hands and knees and demonstrate some maneuvers!

Gotcha

Have fun with your baby's new ability to push things away. Make it a game of having something come too close (such as a game of "gotcha") and show him how to push away the object. Baby will learn how to push things away when he doesn't want something. Remember that the movement is an early form of communication and isn't a negative gesture.

Hammering it up

Babies at this stage will love "hammering" on objects, and it's really a good hand-eye motor skill to learn. Create a hammer out of materials you already have at home, such as a toilet paper roll, a potato chip can, or even a cup and show baby how to use it as a tool to hammer and bang on things. Mark a bull's eye on a sheet of paper, and have your tot use his hammer to hit the target!

En pointe

Flat foot, pointed toe. Babies can point their toes, but parents can help them with the transition from a flexed position to a pointed toe position. Who knows? You may have a future ballet dancer on your hands! You can also show your baby how to kick up and down with straight legs (such as scissor kicks). Not only is this an early exercise, but it helps build leg muscles he'll be using soon enough.

Wastebasket ball

Show your baby how to throw a ball into a basket using a baby-friendly ball. Rubber balls are fun, and babies may just laugh when the ball bounces around and doesn't go into the container, or when it makes a thud as it goes in and stays. While the skill won't yet be developed, you can let your baby have a try at throwing a ball.

Finger pointing

As baby develops fine motor skills, activities that once weren't possible become easy, practically overnight. Show your baby how to point her finger and teach her what it means (i.e., point to a book). Comprehension may come before vocalization, so encourage her to point to her nose, her toes, and of course, to mom and dad!

Pushin' it

Provide baby with a stable object to push around the room to assist with walking. It can be as simple as a weighted box or any number of push toys. Be sure baby can't push it into something that could cause things to tumble over onto her!

Practice Makes Perfect

Build your baby's confidence in sitting upright without toppling over by providing lots of "free sitting" time. Laugh off any wobbles.

Sit 'n' toss

Have your baby sit up while you sit across from her. Toss small objects back and forth (a good choice is the plastic, donut-style toy or a plastic ball about the size of a tennis ball). Toss it to baby so it lands just in front of her to encourage reaching, grasping, and then throwing.

A Frisbee is also a great object to toss back and forth. Use a Styrofoam plate for some simple Frisbee fun. If you prefer, cut out the middle section to create a ring style Frisbee that can also be tossed back and forth. The motion of tossing a Frisbee is great for building hand-eye coordination. You might be surprised at baby's growing strength at this stage!

Angel wings

You don't need snow for this activity. While baby is on his back, encourage him to extend his straightened arms out to each side and raise and lower them. A parent can also hold baby's legs and open and close them while his arms move.

Let's get dressed

It's early yet for your baby to master getting dressed, but encourage him to take on and off simple shoes, hold his arms out, or even to put on a hat. Pulling a shirt over his head is harder, as is pulling on pants. Be very positive and enthusiastic about dressing, and your baby will show developing interest in this skill.

Lids on, lids off

Whoever would have thought plasticware could be so much fun? Let your baby have fun with plastic storage containers and with putting the lids on and taking them off. Make it more fun by tucking a few baby-friendly items inside the storage containers as a surprise!

Also save those shoe boxes for hours of fun. Your baby will love to stack them, take the lids off and put them back on, put things in them, try to sort lids with boxes, and he can even turn them into push toys and race cars.

Wiffle ball

Find a wiffle ball (plastic ball with holes in it) that baby can explore by putting his fingers in the holes and throwing it. The ball won't go far because of its design.

Repetition games

Your baby may thrive on repetition of certain things (that's how he learns). It may be somewhat annoying for you to do the same thing again and again, but you'll be more patient in knowing that baby learns by repeating things over and over.

Your baby will love to pour things out of a container and then (maybe) pick them up and put them back, only to do it again and again. Find a small cloth bag or something similar that is lightweight, and create a dump and pour bag for your baby. Small blocks work well (they won't roll away like balls). This is an activity bag you can take on the go—and baby may try to carry it as well.

Line 'Em Up

Encourage your baby to reach, grab, and place objects into a row for an interesting line up!

Straw zone

Some parents start teaching their babies to drink from a straw before their first year is up, so now is a good time to try. Be sure baby doesn't put the whole straw in his mouth (just the end, of course). For practice, load a favorite drink into the straw while keeping a finger on one end and then let baby suck out the liquid from the other end. Some sippy cup designs feature a built-in straw.

Family fun

My cabinet

You spend so much time in the kitchen, it should come as no surprise that baby will spend time there too! Clean out a lower cabinet or drawer and make it baby's own. Fill it with baby-friendly kitchen items such as large plastic measuring spoons and bowls and let him play while you prepare a meal. Limit his items to just a few so you won't have a mess to clean up (and when he is older, another game can be to put the items away!).

Strollin' along

If you haven't used this parent-loving device much yet, it's time to really bring it out and put those stroller wheels to good use. And because baby is no longer a bobble-head, there's less of a need for "propping," which makes stroller activity more fun for baby and adults alike.

Mom and dad should alternate turns pushing baby in the stroller around the neighborhood or somewhere close and safe, so that baby becomes used to either parent doing the driving. Both parents can walk while baby strolls and point out simple things, such as houses, birds, cars, etc. If possible, build strolls into an every day or several days a week routine. You want baby to get used to the stroller now so there won't be resistance later.

Stretch with Baby

Have baby join you for morning or evening stretching exercises. Simple arm stretches such as reaching for the sky, turning to the side while in the sitting position, neck rolls, and toe touches are more fun when done together. Start a health routine now with baby, and these good habits could stay with him for life.

Bath time car wash

Let baby watch, or even participate (in a baby-safe way), in a family car-washing event. Then pick out a couple of inexpensive plastic cars that baby can call her own and let her wash them during bath time. Practice sequencing events with her, such as starting off with soap, then rinsing, and then drying.

Water hose wonders

Your baby will have a blast with a water hose on a warm day. Allow only a very small trickle of water, but under close supervision let your baby explore the hose and to douse herself with water. Watch how she tries to explore the water's source.

Silly willies

Encourage cases of the "silly willies" by revving up baby for some serious fun! Tell your baby that it's silly willy time, and then proceed to make faces, take baby for a goofy spin around the living room as your dancing partner, or blow fish kisses on her tummy. Have a laugh off! You'll soon find that just telling her that it's "silly willy time!" will invoke a case of the giggles!

Tug of war

Introduce baby to a friendly game of tug-of-war. Use a small towel or similar soft item and engage baby in a slow-motion game of push and pull.

Wildlife walk

Babies at this stage are often interested in holding onto small toys and objects. This is a good age to find some baby-safe plastic animals (farm animals, zoo varieties, or dinosaurs are always popular), and provide baby with a collection to play with as well as something to put them in for on-the-go times. Introduce baby to all the different animals and make their sounds, and encourage him to mimic back. Line them up single-file or side by side. Create an animal parade on the floor one evening and let him knock them down, if he likes!

Blanket ride

Place your baby on a blanket, then pull it around slowly and carefully for a blanket ride. Be sure the ride is on carpet or a safe surface, and that baby doesn't tumble off.

Animal parade

Have your baby create an animal parade with some of his favorite stuffed animals or toys. He can create the parade on his stroller tray or bouncer seat so he can move along with them!

Toy exchange

Remember that babies don't need a lot of different toys to entertain them; in fact, too many toys can overwhelm or even frustrate them. Consider having a toy exchange with families who have similar-aged tots, so babies can experience a "new" toy without accumulating so many of their own that they begin to loose interest. Make it a casual play date and have participants bring two or three toys that they would like to exchange. It's great on the pocketbook, too!

Dad's shoes

Let your baby try to put on dad's big shoes or boots for fun and see what big shoes he will need to fill in coming years! This is a precious photo opportunity as well!

Tissue paper

Making sure he doesn't put it in his mouth, give your baby some tissue paper and show him how to crinkle it, tear it, throw it, and just have some good ol' fun with it! Babies often love the texture combined with bright colors and the ability to wad it up or throw it in the air and watch it float down.

Choo-choo train

Sit behind your baby with legs extended frontward and outside his body, and have your baby become a train engineer! Start making chugging sounds and then make moving motions with your baby as you go up the hills, and then down, fast and slow. You can keep your baby safe by the way you are positioned, and your baby will certainly love these train rides!

Arts and crafts

Ink stamper

Introduce your baby to a child friendly ink stamper. There are many plastic products featuring simple shapes and colors with ink built right into the stamper, and these are easiest to use with baby. Lay down a piece of paper and stamp some designs for baby's viewing and approval. If the stamper uses washable ink, stamp the top of his hand so he can see the design (you can always wash it right off if he protests).

Popsicle stick creatures

Cut out some simple shapes, colors, or animals from a magazine and glue them to the ends of wooden Popsicle sticks (you can purchase wider types from any craft store). Your baby will enjoy holding them and using them for simple play and interaction.

Food art

Using some pureed food as paint, let your baby food paint outdoors in a mess-containing environment. Imagine the palette you can create with carrots (orange), peas (green), and the array of desserts. Pour the food into bowls and then take the art lesson away from the kitchen table and high chair, so baby doesn't associate the food with the art lesson come future meals. Then, let your baby create a masterpiece on a cookie sheet, big piece of paper, or whatever inspires her . . . and you won't mind that she finds the whole experience finger licking fun!

Paper bag puppet

Create very simple puppets using a lunch-size paper bag. Glue on some features such as large google eyes, add ears or other interest items out of foam paper, or use a marker, and show your baby how to use puppets to talk and interact. Make a puppet for you and one for her, and then have a silly conversation (even if it's mostly just sounds)!

Let the Games Begin!

Games and activities for 9 to 12 months

To your baby, life is one big game of hide and seek, and go-go-go. This is such a fun stage, and for parents, it's time to let the games begin!

Your baby is now crawling, maybe even pulling up or standing alone, and for a few babies, beginning to walk. She likes to shake, bang, throw, and of course put everything in her mouth, and finds almost everything amusing (for a few seconds, anyway). This is such a fun stage, and for parents, it's time to let the games begin!

While the world still revolves around baby, your child is also becoming more aware of other tots and adults beyond mom and dad. While parents shouldn't expect their baby to socialize with others much, it is a good time to start teaching babies early socialization skills and concepts such as sharing.

Even before baby officially celebrates a first birthday, most moms and dads realize their helpless and tiny infant has literally transformed into an active and sometimes even temperamental toddler. The first year has just flown by, and the sometimes challenging but always exciting second year awaits. Here are fun and educational activities moms and dads can do in celebration of a look back and a leap ahead!

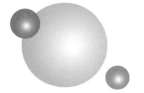

Seeing

Something's fishy

Babies find fish mesmerizing. Why do you think so many doctors' waiting areas feature an aquarium? Visit your local pet store, and let your baby marvel over the fish, or if you're willing, consider buying a single beta fish with a colorful hue that baby can watch. It's a good way to calm an irritable baby, too!

Sight visit

Take your baby on a "sight visit" to somewhere . . . anywhere . . . that you can explore together! Point out various sights and be sure to label them by name. Promote baby's interest in her growing world by visiting various places (plan a few extra minutes on your next errand and let your baby look around).

Are those my toes?

Snap photos of your baby's different body parts (or clip images from a magazine) and place them into a small album. Go through photos with your tot regularly to encourage recognition of different parts of the body. Ask her, "Do you see the photo of your toes? Your mouth? Your nose?" As your baby progresses, ask her to flip through the album and find the photo of her toes, etc.

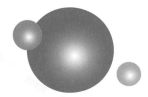

Outdoor explorer

An entire world of new discoveries is just outside baby's door. Now that she's a bit older, take her on an outdoor expedition!

Put your baby on your shoulders (while holding on carefully to her arms), and encourage her curiosity by letting her peek over a fence or other areas she might not normally be able to view outside. Be sure to talk enthusiastically about what you both see.

Introduce your little one to some of the critters she may encounter outside. She will likely find insects and bugs quite interesting. So as to not cause any fright with flapping wings, etc., start with an earthworm hunt after it rains. Let baby watch the worms wriggle and move around. Daring parents might even pick one up for a close-up view by baby! (It's best to avoid having baby touch it.)

Go on a nature walk and let baby feel the grass, touch leaves (even crumble them if it's the right season), smell flowers, and touch the bark of the tree.

When the sun goes down, take your baby for a night-time stroll in a well-lit place, and show her all the pretty lights. Point out the lit signs, street lamps, storefronts, and even blinking attractions.

Headband creations

Create some silly headbands using either colored paper or foam paper to create some one-of-a-kind headbands for baby to wear (and to look at herself in). Simply cut a strip of paper at the right length to go around the circumference of your baby's head and then tape it closed. Next, attach some silly paper designs such as hearts, antlers, clovers, alien or bunny ears, or whatever the season brings and let baby check out her new image!

Magazine marvel

Encourage your baby to sit and look through magazines you receive at home (circulars and catalogs work well too). Use it as a type of picture book—let your baby look over pictures of familiar objects, toys, clothing, or even other smiling toddlers. Have her point out items of interest and use it as a learning moment. Some babies develop a fondness for a certain type of magazine that they enjoy carrying around and "reading" (such as animal or toy catalogs).

Parts and pieces

Your baby may now become interested in objects with parts or pieces, and may even stare at them as if trying to figure out how they work. Find baby-safe objects with two or three pieces that connect, stack, or otherwise come together and introduce them. If your baby doesn't yet seem interested, put it away for a few weeks and then try again.

Go fish

Play a simple fishing game using a pencil, string, and tape along with simple paper or foam shapes that can act as "catches of the day." Construct a fishing pole by taping or tying the string to the end of the pencil. Then place a loop of tape at the end of the string and have your baby dangle it over an edge. Tell him he's fishing. Attach a simple shape or object to the piece of tape and let him see what he caught. Encourage your baby to look at it while you tell him what it is ("That's a red circle," for example), before he casts his line and fishes again!

Photo puzzles

Find a few photos of baby's favorite people or pets and make color copies of the photos. Then cut the copied photos into simple two- or three-piece puzzle shapes, and help your baby put the photo puzzles together. Your tot will delight in seeing a familiar image emerge from the pieces!

Sticker sensation

Let your baby have fun creating a simple scene or picture using tot-friendly stickers. Some stickers are easy-to-peel off with little hands and can be reused on laminate-type sticker books. Find stickers that can be used to create settings (such as house and sun and clouds) or stickers of kids that you can dress (put sticker shoes on the feet, for example).

Or for a simple game, pick up some bright colored sticker dots (usually in the office supply section), and have a dot exchange with your baby. Spread out two or three colors of dots and have your baby follow your lead. Say, "I'm putting a red dot on my leg. Now you get a red dot. Can you put it on your leg?" Let your baby pick a dot color (you say its color out loud) and then follow his lead as to where it is put.

Book backpack

Place a few age-appropriate books in a baby backpack or bag that your child can carry around on car trips and adventures. Change out books often and tuck in a small surprise to encourage baby to stay interested in his very own book backpack.

Happy/sad

Show your baby basic facial expressions, such as "happy face," "sad face," and "mad face," and encourage her to mimic each expression back to you. Reinforce her growing knowledge of feelings and faces by saying things such as, "What a great happy face you have on this morning!" or "Why the sad face today?"

Karate kid

While holding onto your baby to avoid any tumbles, encourage him to make some simple kicking motions first with one foot and then another. As baby feels more comfortable, show him how to really extend the entire leg and to try simple lunges (still with your support). You may have a future karate kid on your hands!

Hearing

First books

Encourage your baby to listen as you read simple books. If possible, choose books with interactive features such as textures to feel, buttons to push, or tabs to pull. The best types feature thick pages with a laminate coating so pages won't get ripped or chewed on! Ask your baby simple questions about the book, such as "Do you see a sheep? Can you show me the sheep you see on this page? Do you know what a sheep says? It says *baaahhh*. Can you say that?"

Cardboard sticks

Turn your empty paper towel or toilet paper rolls into some safe banging sticks for baby. Show him how to bang the two together to make a noise. It's okay to whack them together because the soft cardboard will prevent any harm from being done.

Whimsical sounds

Whether it's a pop, whirl, screech, hiss, or snort, have fun with some nonsensical sounds for some listening fun. Who knows? Your baby may create a few of his own in return! You can also tap out some simple beats with your feet or fingers on a hard surface, and encourage your baby to listen to the beat and repeat it back!

Can baby respond?

Make a simple request to your baby and see whether he understands and responds. Try something similar to "Get your shoes" or "Can you wave bye-bye to Grandma?" Be sure to speak simply and keep it to a single request, and above all, make sure you have baby's attention before gauging a response.

Further encourage your baby's listening skills by asking him questions that earn a response. For example, "Where's the cat? Do you see kitty?" Watch as your baby looks around; this is your cue that he both heard you as well as understood what you asked.

Animal Associations

Engage in some silly animal sounds with baby, like a cat's meow or dog's bark, and then say the animal's name.

Quack quack!

Cut out pictures of animals and then teach your child their corresponding sounds. Ask your tot to show you the picture of the animal that says "bow wow!" or "quack quack!" Start with only two or three animals, and then add more as your child develops.

Sound check

Take baby on a sound expedition throughout your home (indoors or out) and let her hear all the household noises, including some that are brand new! Turn faucets on and off, open and close doors, flush the toilets, knock on the front door, open a window, and even open and close your refrigerator. Remember that even though these sounds may be mundane to you, they are ever-interesting to your tot's sharp hearing.

Sound off

By this stage, your baby can make all sorts of sounds and maybe even a few words. Have a sound-off contest in which you make a sound, baby mimics it, and back and forth. Let baby lead, if he likes. Imitation is a great source of fun and is a teaching tool as well.

Follow the Beat

Tap out some simple beats with your feet or fingers on a hard surface, and encourage your baby to listen to the beat and repeat it back!

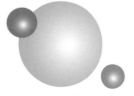

Touch

Drawer full of fun

Earmark a drawer for baby that she can open and close, allowing her to add and pull out baby-safe objects for play and exploration. Include some objects that are fun to feel, such as squishy balls, powder puffs, bath loofahs, etc.

More than a feeling

Give your baby some interesting textures to feel, and label each with a word to describe the sensation. Sandpaper is "rough," while a glue stick is "sticky," and an ice cube is "cold." Some squishy toys (water worms or squishy balls are examples) are fun to introduce at this stage, but parental supervision is required.

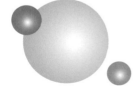

Water fun

Give your baby a bucket or two of water and some plastic cups, and let the play begin! Your baby will enjoy the feeling of water (make it room temperature) and like pouring and splashing, although she may or may not like getting all wet!

Pick and pull

Whether it's picking a wild flower or pulling up some grass, show your baby how to pick an object by pulling. Some babies like to sit in the grass just to feel it and pull on it, while others don't like the texture at all. Clover can also be fun to pick (just make sure no plants end up in the mouth!).

Foam soap

Let your baby feel foam soap. She'll find the texture interesting and you can make hand washing a fun experience using one of the many baby-friendly soap products on the market. Let her casually dip a hand into a foam pile or squish it between her hands.

Ice interest

Let your baby touch an ice cube or play with some crushed ice. She may find the coldness interesting, especially on a warm weather day. Freeze some shapes and let her watch them melt.

Oatmeal dough

Make natural dough your baby can safely play with, using ingredients from your pantry.

Ingredients:
 1 cup flour
 2 cups oatmeal
 1 cup water

Mix flour and oatmeal in a bowl and then gradually add water. Knead until mixed, adding dry or wet ingredients until desired texture is reached. Show baby how to play with the dough as modeling clay.

Rainy day feeling

Grab an umbrella and let your baby experience rain. Pick a soft, light rainy day when it's safe to be outdoors. Let your baby feel the raindrops with his hand. Later, when the rain stops, let him go outdoors and play in a puddle.

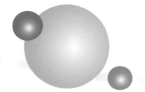

Sloshy entertainment

Whoever would have thought that a Ziploc bag and water could provide so much entertainment? Fill a quart-size baggie about halfway full with water and zip it close. Then place the filled bag into a second baggie to avoid any unanticipated leaks. While under adult supervision, let your baby hold the sloshy bag and even shake it and grab it. Many babies will be intrigued with its slippery texture. Parents can show baby how the water can be squished from side to side.

Junk mail

Let your baby get the mail, and then after sorting through it, let him try his skill at opening the unwanted (junk) mail. You may need to open the envelope, but baby will feel ever-so-important helping you with this essential household duty every day!

Taste and smell

Bath scents

Add a small amount of scent to baby's bath water or to a small cup that baby can sniff. Baking extracts are safe, and peppermint or vanilla are good choices. You can also use scented baby bath products and encourage your baby to smell them.

More First Words

Identify smells and tastes for your baby ("Smell this, baby? Doesn't it smell really sweet?") to help baby associate words with tastes and smells as soon as she is able.

Ice cream lickin'

Put on an old shirt and introduce your baby to the art of licking an ice-cream cone (pending any dietary restrictions). Licking an ice-cream cone is a learned activity, so don't be surprised if most of the ice cream ends up down the front of baby's shirt or around her mouth. Be sure to get a cone yourself and show baby how it's done!

Fascinating sippy cup

One way to foster a smooth transition from bottle to sippy cup is to introduce the cup as a fascinating new object that is baby's to hold, taste, and use, while at the same time making the bottle seem less exciting. Try a sippy cup with handles or exciting designs. Make a big fuss over baby's cup and any interest shown toward it, but don't expect an immediate changeover.

Spaghetti science

Cook up some spaghetti, let it cool off, and then allow your baby to play with it (and eat some too, if she's interested). Many babies will find the spaghetti's texture interesting and enjoy exploring it with their hands. Experiment with different types of pasta (bow-tie, shells, penne, etc.) and see which shape baby prefers.

Fruit Popsicle

Make a homemade Popsicle for baby by pouring fruit juice (it can be diluted with water, if you prefer) into an ice cube tray. When the mixture gets slushy, add a Popsicle stick or other type of handle and freeze. Place your baby into her high chair, or weather permitting, take her outside and provide her with an icy-cold snack. If baby seems reluctant, consider breaking the Popsicle into small pieces.

Have Patience with Picky Eaters

At this stage, your baby probably has a definite preference for certain foods. Don't be too discouraged if she only likes one or two foods, just keep introducing foods with a variety of tastes and textures (with your pediatrician's approval), and your baby will expand her likes (as well as dislikes) with time.

Plant nursery visit

Plan a short trip to a plant nursery and let your baby smell the flowers, see and feel the different types of foliage, and admire the blooms.

O stacks

Ahh, the fun a baby can have with Cheerios or other "O"- shaped cereals! Stir sticks provide a great opportunity for a baby to practice stacking. With you holding a stir stick upright, encourage your baby to stack the cheerios on top of one another.

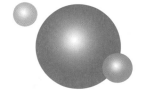

Language development

Baby on tape

Use a recorder (tape, video, or even a digital camera that can capture a short clip), and encourage your baby to make silly sounds or form first words. Play it back for baby to hear. As she begins to understand that she is listening to her own voice, her animation, babbles, or early words may increase.

Nonsense Never Sounded So Good!

Encourage your baby to vocalize by turning it into a game. Offer significant praise when your baby says a word or tries to (babbling and gibberish are early words . . . she knows what she's saying; you just don't!)

Finger pop

Your baby will think it is too funny when you pop your finger out of the side of your mouth and make that "popping" sound. It provides for some silly impromptu entertainment! Don't be surprised if she tries to mimic the sound back!

Karaoke: baby style

Show your baby how to sing into a plastic cup, so her voice amplifies. Change pitches and encourage your youngster to mimic the highs and lows of singing. Start with simple one-syllable sounds such as "la-la-la" and then progress as your baby's voice develops.

Or, craft a simple "microphone" from a paper towel or toilet paper roll and show your baby how to use it to amplify noises. Be silly and show her how to sing into it like a performer.

You can also make an audio or video recording of these early vocalizations to play back for baby. Watch her reaction! Simple recordings such as these can become a treasure that you'll keep for years.

What's that?

Choose a baby-friendly "pointing stick" (a plastic straw works great) and let baby explore her environment by pointing at things. Show how her how to point and ask any variation of "what's that?" When you answer her, have her repeat the object's name to the best of her speaking ability.

Keep It Simple

Your baby may now understand simple commands, with "no" quickly rising to the top of the list. When you vocalize a command, make sure you keep it short and direct ("No! Hot!" for example).

Who's calling?

Babies love playing on the telephone, so get her a toy variety and practice saying hello. Get two and have phone conversations . . . baby style!

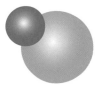

Motor development

Reach and balance

This activity may be more appropriate earlier, or later, depending on which stage of development your baby is in. When your youngster can stand alone, encourage him to balance by having him reach up with both arms, and then extend them outward. Have him touch his shoulders, nose, and top of head while standing. Be sure there's nothing around that he could tumble into if he loses balance.

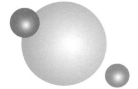

First sports

Play some kickball, parent style! Have one parent hold baby upright at the waist while the other parent (or other adult) slowly rolls a ball toward baby. Encourage baby to kick the ball back. It's a great way to develop early coordination and kicking efforts, and it's just plain fun!

Is your little one a future bowler? Using plastic cups as bowling pins and a small ball (such as a tennis ball), show your baby how to roll a ball into the cups with the goal of knocking them over. Cheer for baby when she gets a strike!

Play an early form of T-Ball by placing a small plastic ball on a stand made from an empty toilet paper roll. Let your baby swat it off, using either his hand or with a small "bat" made from a paper towel roll or plastic tube. Be sure to cheer with every direct hit!

Create a Healthy Routine

Get your baby moving. Minimize the time spent in a stroller, swing, or high chair and encourage him to "move it, move it" with you in tow. Keep your baby active, curious, and on the go whether it is a walk, crawl, creep, or movement that is uniquely his own.

Scoop it up

Give baby some balls that she can hold in her hand, and show her how to put them in a basket or container. Start with two or three balls, preferably of different colors. As baby scoops one up, tell her, "Great! You got the red ball. Now place it in the basket!"

Work those arms!

Teach your baby an easy cheer involving arm motions. You can say the words, and baby can extend her arms while in a seated position and give an ol' "rah, rah!" Consider it fun with exercise and motor development built right in!

Or show your baby how to extend her arms like a plane and take her on an exciting flight by lifting her at the waist, soaring in the sky. When baby is able to walk, you can have the big plane lead the small plane on all sorts of adventures.

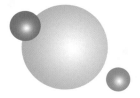

Size sorter

Baby can learn how to sort sizes using items you already have readily available at home. Find three different sized containers (think small, medium, and large) and then find three different sized objects as well. Demonstrate how objects can all fit into certain containers but how a large object won't fit into a small container. Let her try it herself.

Royal baby

Craft a simple crown out of paper, adding some glitter or colorful personalized touches if you like. Then let baby watch as you ceremoniously place it on her head!

Without any assistance baby should be waving bye-bye by now (assuming she's interested, of course). Especially outgoing babies may even have their own style of wave. Have fun with baby's wave by showing her the distinguished "queen's royal wave."

Basket of fun

Place a few objects nearby your tot, give him a basket (a lightweight cloth type is best) and show him how to pick things up and put them in the basket. Once they are gathered, encourage him to put them back out for you to pick up.

First candle

In preparation for the momentous milestone of turning one and blowing out a first candle (if you observe this custom), have your baby practice blowing one out! It's harder than you think, and the act of huffing and then blowing is something that babies don't initially understand. If you show the skill and then practice, your baby may be ready when the real birthday arrives!

Baby bop

If your baby is walking, engage in some silly dance fun! If she's not walking yet, have her stand up on your legs facing you and do some bop and swing moves! Find an upbeat, fast-paced song you both love and make "bopping" a fun activity you enjoy on a regular basis.

Or place baby's feet on top of yours and enjoy some couple dancing. Your tot will like the sensation of you controlling the dance moves while you hold onto her arms. Slowly step side to side, front to back, and then if your baby seems receptive, add some twirls and dips into the mix!

Boys and girls alike will enjoy toe tapping to the beat of music. If your baby can stand or hold onto an object and tap a toe or heel onto the ground, great! If not, just have him sit or hold him between your legs and encourage toe and heel tap exercises onto the floor. Certain shoes may even have a "clack" sound to add to the fun, but the key is to exercise control of toe and heel onto a surface while maintaining a sense of balance.

Try putting on some Polynesian-inspired music, and show your baby a basic hula dance. Have fun gently waving arms and moving hips, and swaying to the tune.

Duck waddle walk

If your baby is walking, walking with support, or crawling with gusto, show your baby silly waddle walks like a duck. Flap your arms and make quacking sounds and have your baby mimic back.

> ### Rock Star
>
> **Get on all fours alongside your baby and show him how to rock back and forth. Put on some playful music and turn it into an early exercise game!**

Take a bow

Teach your baby to take a bow after a great performance. Bowing is an act of balance, and it's a new skill your star performer will use often!

Obstacle course

Set up a safe and simple obstacle course for baby, depending on his developmental level. It can be as simple as crawling over a cushion or under a chair. You can increase the challenge depending on baby's current stage.

Toddlers Love to Choose

Your baby is quickly progressing to an independent-minded toddler, and so parents should encourage decision-making and selection skills. Maybe it's letting your baby choose between two pairs of shoes (even putting a simple pair on) or asking him to get you a diaper when he needs changing. His gross and fine motor skills have made extraordinary strides these twelve months, and there is so much more your toddler can do today.

Family fun

Wash and dry

Using two big plastic tubs (one with soap and one for rinsing), let your baby wash some plastic dishes, and even dry them off afterward. If weather permits, set up your dishwashing station outside. Your baby will like the chance to participate in pretending to wash dishes, rinse, and then dry them off. Who knows? Maybe she'll do it for real when older!

Get Out and Play

While true interactive play won't yet occur at this stage, baby's social skills are starting to emerge. Seek out parents with similar-age babies and start a casual play group for stimulation and social development. Mom and dad will enjoy the time with other parents as much as the babies will with each other!

Object hide 'n' seek

Babies become really curious by this stage of development. Simple object hiding games are a prefect way to tickle baby's newfound urge to explore.

Take a simple paper bag and place an object inside. Ask baby, "What's in the bag?" Let her look inside and remove the object. Make it a regular game by changing out objects, small toys, or even adding in an occasional treat as well!

Introduce your tot to the game of hide 'n' seek, but instead of hiding yourselves, hide an object. Show your baby how you can hide something, have everyone else look for it, and then everyone gets to shout "hooray" when it is found. Once baby grasps the concept that something hidden can be found, she'll be ready to play the game of hiding herself as she enters the world of toddlerhood!

Try a simple treasure hunt with baby. It can be as simple as hiding a small item in sand or even in flour or amongst some rocks for baby to discover on his own! Treasure hunts will become more elaborate during his toddler years, but your baby will love the seek and find activity!

Hats off

Have fun with some silly hats, and be sure the camera is close by. Let baby try on oversized hats such as a cowboy hat, baseball cap, or whatever you have around. Let baby put the hats on you too and be sure to strike a silly pose!

Cardboard playhouse

Set a large cardboard box on its side and let baby go in and out of it. If your baby is standing, make sure you are nearby to avoid any spills. Creative parents can fashion a simple cardboard playhouse for baby by cutting a door and even windows. Baby can even decorate her playhouse with crayons or markers.

Balloon toss

Blow up a small balloon and show baby how to swat and toss it into the air and back and forth to you. During warm weather, and depending on your baby's temperament, consider making a water balloon and tossing it back and forth outdoors (best way is to sit on the ground across from each other). Show him how it will break and that water will come out.

Bird watching

Babies are fascinated by birds, so go to the park, your backyard, or wherever there are birds in your area and spend some time bird watching. Count the birds you see, and talk to your baby about birds and how they fly. For extra fun, participate in the annual Great Backyard Bird Count (www.birdsource.org) that engages bird watchers of all ages in counting birds.

Bubble fun

Your almost-toddler will have a blast with bubbles! Buy an inexpensive container of bubbles and blow them around your baby, letting him watch how they float and pop. She might even enjoy waving her hands through them as they soar nearby. Some babies may even be able to blow through a wand to form a bubble . . . try it and see!

Family superheroes

Don towels or sheets on family members, including your baby, and have everyone act like a caped crusader. Your baby won't understand superheroes at this stage, but will indeed love getting to "fly" (with adult help) and acting silly along with mom and dad!

Rice sandbox

Your baby will love playing with his own sandbox. Place uncooked rice in a box or bucket and add a few cups or shovels (measuring cups work well). Most babies like the texture and coolness of rice, and it is fun to dump and pour. Place a plastic liner or cookie tray underneath for easy clean-up.

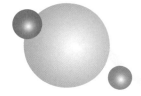

Fun at the table

Your tot should now have most of the skills needed to set a table (at least a pretend one) using paper plates and plastic silverware and cups. Even if your baby is not yet walking, you can create a mini table that she can set up. It will make her feel like a big girl!

The table can also be a great place to play! When mealtime is over, of course, your baby will find it so much fun to get under the table with you. The two of you can hide from another adult or sibling, or simply enjoy an under-the-table outing, complete with a snack or book.

Wipe out

Give baby a damp cloth or a wet wipe and encourage him to clean along with you. Pick something simple to clean (many babies like to "clean" their high chair tray, for example). You can also give your baby a mini dustpan and brush, and he'll have fun helping you to sweep and clean.

Arts and crafts

Photo treasures

Tuck photos of family, friends, and pets into a small plastic album (4 × 6 size works great) that baby can look through as an activity. Sit with her and point out loved ones. Ask her to find the photo of "mama" or "dad." In time, she will!

Frown buster

Create a "frown box" (a shoebox works great) and the next time your tot gets pouty or wears a big frown, take him on a frown find to lock away those frowns in a box. Look under the table, in the refrigerator, on the couch, and guess what? Be sure to find and take that frown right off his face, put it in a box, and store it in the closet. This fun activity will be certain to turn that frown into one happy smile!

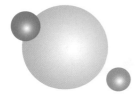

Water painting

Give your baby a paint brush and some water, and let him "paint" outdoors. No color or canvas is required for some natural fun . . . and there is no mess to clean up!

Finger Fun

Find some cheap cotton or plastic gloves and cut off the fingers to make some simple finger characters. For extra interest, use pipe cleaners or even markers to create your finger characters. Let baby watch as your "fingers" talk, sing, dance and move.

Little wizard

Create some silly wands using a straw and paper and maybe some curly ribbon, if desired. Let your baby wave the wand around or even cast spells! Your toddler may not yet understand wizards or princesses, but will love being able to hold a pretty object and wave it around.

Yogurt art

Let your baby "finger paint" with yogurt on a plate (a white paper plate is best). If you or baby prefers, he can also paint with a new child's paintbrush. Show baby how to mix up a color and then create simple artwork on the plate using his hands or paintbrush.

Simple flashcards

Who needs to purchase flashcards for a baby when you can make some simple ones yourself? Just buy a packet of 3×5 index cards and display some basic shapes and colors on the cards. Or, find and glue on photos of family members. Have your child look over the cards while you identify the objects that are shown. As your baby matures, start laying out a few at a time and ask her to pick the object you say. (For example, ask her point to the flashcard with the color blue or the one that has a picture of Nana.)

A Year of Firsts

There's always a reason or season to celebrate!

Here are some seasonal celebrations and holiday happenings to enjoy with your baby over the course of the first year.

Winter

Candy cane smiles

Age permitting, give your baby a small candy cane and show her how to lick it for some sticky smiles. Many babies like the taste and smell of peppermint, and the holiday treat is an indulgence that promises some photo fun (have some wet wipes nearby). Just be sure baby doesn't stick the candy too far in her mouth, and break off any sharp edges.

Santa Baby

Start an annual tradition of Santa and Baby photos. Consider buying a special Santa hat that will be worn for every year's photo for a sentimental touch. When the tradition ends, put all the photos in chronological order into a special Santa Baby book that will promise to become one of your family's most prized holiday possessions.

Happy New Year Baby

Your baby only officially gets one occasion to celebrate Baby New Year, so make it a lasting memory by creating a keepsake photo of your baby clad in only a diaper with a hat or Happy New Year tiara. Silly glasses with the numbers of the New Year can also be worn. Send out your photo to friends and family as a special way to bring in the New Year!

Make baby a colorful wand streamer to celebrate the New Year. Tape a piece of ribbon or crepe paper to a long straw, pencil, or even a chop stick and show your baby how to wave it with gusto.

For a simple noisemaker, decorate a toilet paper tube with markers and ribbons (or however you prefer) and then wrap a small cellophane circle over one end of the tube and secure with rubber bands. Show your tot how to hold the open end of the tube up to her mouth and make noises. This same craft idea makes a great noisemaker to celebrate your baby's first birthday as well!

Valentine hearts

Make your baby thumbprint hearts for Valentine's Day or any time you want her to have a special "signature" on a card. Press her thumb into red washable paint and then onto paper. You'll need two thumbprints for each heart, overlapping the print at the bottom and angling outward to form the heart shape. After you're done, you can wash her thumb, and you'll have a heart keepsake!

Or, simply cut a heart shape out of construction paper. With your baby's help (even if it is just a dab), use a washable marker or paint to create simple markings. Place a special photo of your baby in the center of the heart and give to loved ones.

Shamrock glasses

Fold a piece of green foam paper in half and cut out a shamrock with one end on the fold, so that when the paper is unfolded there are two connecting shamrock shapes that will become eye glasses. Cut out the middle of the shapes for eyeholes. Poke a small hole on each side of the glasses and tie a piece of green yarn through each hole. Tie the glasses on safely behind baby's head for some St. Patrick's Day fun.

Spring

Baby garden

Set aside a certain part of your yard for your baby's own garden. With your baby watching (or helping, if she's old enough), you can plant a few plants or flowers. She can help to water them (with a plastic baby water container, of course) and observe how things grow. Each year, replant items in the special area and you may create a kid with a natural green thumb!

Easter egg hunt

You don't even need to put anything into the plastic eggs; just letting your infant "hunt" for eggs for the first time and placing them into a basket is memorable enough! This is an activity that can be enjoyed year-round, regardless of the season, and encourages motor skills of reaching, grasping, and putting into a container.

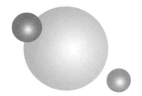

Family egg fun

Decorate hard-boiled eggs (one for each member of your family). Use markers, glitter, glue, yarn for hair, etc., and let your baby have a plastic egg of her own to play with at the same time. Take a photo of your egg family and make this an annual tradition. When your baby is old enough, let her create an egg likeness on her own.

Kite Flying fancy

Celebrate spring by flying a kite for your baby's wonder and amusement. Your tot will enjoy the outdoors and watching a kite soar in the wind. A simple one with a long colorful tail will hold her interest best.

Puddle jumper

Have a puddle jumping contest after a spring rain, and let your baby play in puddles and experience the fun that comes after a rainfall! It is fine if an extra pair of adult hands assist with the jumps through the puddles. And, if it's warm enough, forget the rain boots or shoes; let her wiggle her tootsies in the water or splash to her heart's content!

Rainbow of fun

Cut out a rainbow shape, color it in with bright colors, and make your baby's own pot of gold at the end of the rainbow for a first-year tradition. The rainbow's "treasure" can yield a new toy, stuffed animal, snack, or even a special family outing! The leprechaun is something that can be taught another year.

Some bunny special

Craft some simple bunny ears out of paper using markers and glitter, cut out according to shape, and then either tuck them into your baby's headband or tape onto a hat. Position your baby in a field of flowers or other spring setting and capture that first Easter portrait! Creative parents can even draw on a bunny nose and whiskers for effect!

Summer

Dancing with the stars

Plan a summer starlight outing with your baby that involves dancing with (under) the stars. Bring out some music and have a family outing on a warm summer night that involves fun tunes and family dancing. Be as silly as you like (your baby just loves a twirl around!).

Day at the beach

You don't have to go to the ocean for a fun day at the beach with your baby. Purchase a bag or two of sand and place in a large bucket. Give your baby a pail, scoop, or sand toys of choice and let her have an afternoon of sand fun. Show your baby how to bury her toes (or yours) in the sand.

Flag waving

Create a simple flag out of paper strips and construction paper and then attach it to a dowel stick (with rounded ends) or even a sturdy straw and let your baby have a flag waving time for a special occasion. You can create simple flags for important holidays or special occasions.

Ice melter

Freeze some juice in ice cube tray, inserting a wooden stick when the juice is slushy enough to hold it upright. When the cubes are frozen, have a summer celebration in the backyard with your own cool snack.

Parade of babies

Decorate your baby's wagon or stroller (depending on the weather and your baby's age) using balloons and ribbons. Invite your friends with kids, and have a baby parade. You can organize a parade around the Fourth of July holiday or any season and any reason works as well. You could even have a baby parade in celebration of your baby's first birthday, even if it's just a quick stroll around the block.

Umbrella camp out

Don a beach towel, large rain umbrella, some graham crackers if your baby is old enough, and a flashlight and have a mini campout with baby in the backyard.

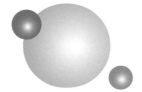

Water slide

Create a simple baby-sized water slide by using a plastic table cloth or something similar. Secure corners with heavy objects and then hose it down with a water hose or spray bottle and let your baby safely slide outdoors for some slippery and cool entertainment.

Dried fruit treats

If your baby can eat fruit, take some of summertime's harvest and turn it into healthy fruit treats. Slice your fruit of choice into thin (about ¼ inch) slices. Small berries can be dried whole. Spread the fruit slices in a single layer on a cookie sheet. Place in a preheated 150 degree oven and dry until the moisture is gone but the fruit is still soft. Note that the fruit will be brown because no preservatives are used, but it will taste great! Place the dried fruit slices into a lidded jar and let them sit tight for at least a week before eating. It makes a tasty treat on the go.

Fall

Fall leaves

Collect some of nature's most beautiful leaves as they fall from the trees and let your baby look at them, feel them, and even smell them! If age allows, introduce your baby to the fun of raking leaves into a bundle and falling into them, or at least kicking some around (even with mom or dad's help!).

Orange jack-o'-lanterns

Create a baby-friendly jack-o'-lantern using an orange with the top cut off and insides scooped out. Draw a happy jack-o'-lantern face on the outside of the face and fill the inside with something on your baby's dietary list (yogurt, ice cream, or even cereal mixture). This is recommended only for babies on solid food.

Pumpkin turkey

Use an uncut pumpkin left over from Halloween, trace your baby's handprint on different pieces of fall-colored construction paper (about six hand prints will be ample for most medium-sized pumpkins) and tape them onto the back in a fan shape to create the tail feathers of a turkey. Next cut out the shape of your baby's foot (in a shoe shape; no need for toes), draw on eyes with the heel portion becoming the head, and tape it to the front of the pumpkin. You now have a unique turkey made from the shapes of your baby's current-sized hands and feet!

Tattoo dress-up

As an alternative to dressing up baby for a fall festival or trick or treat time, consider using temporary tattoos with silly designs. You can add a simple temporary tattoo or two on your baby's cheeks for the "oh so cute" moments without creating any fuss.

Turkey handprint cookies

Trace your baby's hand onto paper and cut out. This will become your shape for cookies. Roll out sugar cookie dough (use prepackaged for a quick and easy way). Cut out cookie dough in accordance with your baby's hand-print pattern. Bake according to directions. When cool, decorate like a turkey by making the thumb serve as neck and head, and the four fingers to become feathers. Ice in whatever color or colors are desired, place an M&M or small candy on the thumb to represent an eye, and then create a pattern on the icing for feathers or use small candies. You'll have one-of-a-kind cookies that will certainly shout, "Gobble, gobble!"

Year of Memories

All in the family

Find a photo of yourself as a baby and of your parents and generations before. A photo grouping of loved ones as babies will be a sure conversation piece in your home. It will also encourage the comparisons of noses, eyes, coloring, and even expressions!

Foot chart

Trace your baby's foot onto colorful foam paper and create a height "foot chart" on an interior door frame. Add your baby's footprints as she grows to denote growth, marking the actual height and date using a permanent marker. As your baby grows, more feet will continue to be added. It's a cute way to show your baby's increasing size as measured in feet!

Handprint wall

Create a handprint wall of your baby's handprints and/or footprints over the first year using colorful child-friendly paint. (The best bet is tempera paint found at craft stores.) Handprints can be added on a door frame, on a wall, or on fabric that can be displayed.

How quickly I grow

Find a constant background for a monthly photo to be taken during your baby's first year. Position your baby in the same way each time. Maybe it's in a certain over-stuffed chair in the living room or in baby's crib. The photos will clearly show your baby's amazing and rapid growth this first year.

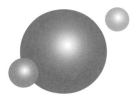

Journal of memories

While most parents have a baby book that records special happenings and milestones, these books don't typically have spaces dedicated to ongoing reflections about baby's first year. A journal can be as simple as a spiral notebook or thoughts written on the computer and then printed out. Honor each month of your baby's first year with an entry into your journal and then tuck those observations into a baby book.

Shoe box time capsule

Create time capsules of each year of your baby's life using simple shoe boxes. Place beloved items inside such as a favorite outfit, a newborn diaper, a well-worn toy, outgrown shoes, a few select photos of your baby throughout the year, and a handwritten note by loved ones. On the final day of each year (or a date of your choosing), pull the box(es) out and look over the contents with your family. Reminiscing of days gone by and how quickly your baby has grown will make these shoe box capsules your dearest keepsakes.

T-Shirt quilt

This is an idea that could take years to complete (depending on your preference), but it is well worth it. Save cute T-shirts from the time your child is a baby up through high school, (or whatever period of time you choose) and cut the T-shirts into squares showcasing the message on the shirt. Stitch the squares together and place them on a solid backing or another blanket of the same size, and you'll have a quilt or a special wall hanging.

Tooth fairy time

Everyone knows that the tooth fairy collects baby teeth that are lost, but why not have a tooth celebration marking the arrival of a first tooth? Create a certificate proclaiming the day your baby's first tooth makes its debut, and be sure to note the exact location so you'll remember it later. When your baby later loses that very tooth, write a note to the tooth fairy asking to keep it for sentimental reasons, and then place that special tooth on display in conjunction with the certificate.

Index by Activity Title

About the Author

Robin McClure is a professional writer as well as a wife and a busy mom of three very active kids. She has served as the About.com Guide to Child Care since 2004 and has worked in the fields of public education and continuing education for fourteen years. Her first book, *The Playskool Toddler's Busy Play Book*, was published in July 2007. She and her family live in North Richland Hills, Texas.

Notes

ISBN: 978-1-4022-0934-5
$14.95 U.S./$19.95 CAN/£7.99 UK

THE PLAYSKOOL

Guide for

Expectant fathers

The information-packed, practical guide to the most exciting time of your life

The Playskool Guide for Expectant Fathers, written by MD (and father of three) Brian Lipps, gives you the advice and information you need to understand what's happening during every step of pregnancy. Most important, you'll learn how to get involved in ways that give you a close and incredible experience while helping mom toward the big day. From communicating with mommy to planning for the future, *The Playskool Guide for Expectant Fathers* answers the questions every dad-to-be (and mom) may have.

- Develop an action plan of things to do to get ready for baby
- Great starting points for many pregnancy-related conversations
- How to support, encourage and help your pregnant partner
- Understand the physical and emotional changes occurring to mom
- Get involved by reading—and talking—to the bump in the belly
- Learn about your baby's month-by-month development

The essential resource for your new adventures in daddyhood

Sourcebooks, Inc.
www.sourcebooks.com

Brian Lipps, MD

ISBN: 978-1-4022-0931-4
$14.95 U.S./$19.95 CAN/£7.99 UK

THE PLAYSKOOL Guide to Baby's first year

The information-packed, practical guide to your baby's wonderful first year

Your baby's first year is filled with new experiences and important choices. Written by MD (and mother of four) Jamie Loehr and teacher and education writer (and mother of two) Jen Meyers, *The Playskool Guide to Baby's First Year* provides essential information and expert advice to help you prepare for baby's arrival and make the right choices for you and your baby. From together time to baby baths, from knowing what to expect to monitoring baby's development, *The Playskool Guide to Baby's First Year* answers the questions and addresses the concerns every mom and dad may have.

- Customizing the birth plan that's right for you
- A month-by-month guide to baby's development
- How to pick a doctor for your baby
- Breastfeeding or formula? How to help baby develop healthy eating habits
- The well-child visits for the first year, including all the developmental milestones
- Strategies for soothing a crying baby and encouraging peaceful sleep
- Playing together and helping baby learn

Essential information, practical advice and key choices for your baby's first 12 months

Sourcebooks, Inc.
www.sourcebooks.com

Jamie Loehr, MD and Jen Meyers

ISBN: 978-1-4022-0932-1
$14.95 U.S./$19.95 CAN/£7.99 UK

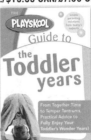

THE PLAYSKOOL Guide to the Toddler years

Welcome to the wonderful world of toddlers—the most amazing time of your child's life!

As your toddler grows and explores the world, every day brings new adventures and bonding opportunities. *The Playskool Guide to the Toddler Years*, filled with caring advice from clinical psychologist Rebecca Rutledge, offers essential, practical information you need to know to ease your fears and parent with confidence! From sleep and teething to developing speech and language, *The Playskool Guide to the Toddler Years* is your indispensable, easy-to-understand guide to handling every aspect of your toddler's growing mind, busy body and emotional well-being.

- Building imagination and learning through play
- Easy guidelines for rules and discipline
- Understanding the important cognitive, physical and emotional changes
- Parenting yourself to maintain your sanity
- Beginning potty training and getting ready for preschool
- Traveling with your toddler
- Socializing with siblings and making new friends

From together time to temper tantrums, practical advice to fully enjoy your toddler's wonder years!

Sourcebooks, Inc.
www.sourcebooks.com

Rebecca Rutledge, PhD

ISBN: 978-1-4022-0933-8
$14.95 U.S./$19.95 CAN/£7.99 UK

THE PLAYSKOOL

Toddler's busy play Book

Play opens a world of creativity, discovery and learning.

With more than 500 activities, games, crafts and recipes for any child or situation and every day of the year, *The Playskool Toddler's Busy Play Book* will give you hours of creative fun, playing, bonding and growing together with your busy toddler! As the American Academy of Pediatrics (AAP) recently reported, play is essential for helping children reach important developmental milestones.

Smart zone–games to stimulate the mind and teach new skills

Fun with the family–great quality-time ideas that get the whole family involved

Play dates–winning activities to captivate a household of rambunctious youngsters

Sick days–keep toddlers from getting fidgety as they rest and recuperate

Travel time–so much fun that kids may forget to ask, "Are we there yet?"

Holiday fun–holiday-themed activities from January to December

Calm and quiet–keeping toddlers busy and quiet when you're out and about or relaxing at home

The Playskool Toddler's Busy Play Book **provides 500 great ways to entertain, teach, amuse and delight your very busy toddler.**

Sourcebooks, Inc.
www.sourcebooks.com

Robin McClure